Eats, Shites & Leaves

CRAP
ENGLISH AND HOW TO USE IT

Eats, Shites & Leaves

CRAP ENGLISH AND HOW TO USE IT

A. PARODY

Michael O'Mara Books Limited

First published in Great Britain in 2004 by
Michael O'Mara Books Limited
9 Lion Yard
Tremadoc Road
London SW4 7NQ

This paperback edition first published in 2007

A CIP catalogue record for this book is available from the British Library

Papers used by Michael O'Mara Books Limited are natural, recyclable
products made from wood grown in sustainable forests. The manufacturing
processes conform to the environmental regulations of the country of origin.

ISBN: 978-1-84317-274-1

10 9 8 7 6 5 4 3 2 1

Designed and typeset by Design 23

Printed and bound in Great Britain by Cox & Wyman, Reading, Berks

Here will be an old abusing of God's patience
and the king's English.
William Shakespeare, *The Merry Wives of Windsor*

Better to trip in with the feet than with the tongue.
Zeno (300 BC)

No one is listening until you make a mistake.
Anonymous

It's like correcting people's grammar – I don't do
it to be popular.
Dr Frasier Crane, *Frasier*

DISCLAIMER!

All spelling and grammatical errors in this book are intentional;
otherwise they were put there by the editor.

> 'No passion in the world is equal
> to the passion to alter
> someone else's draft.'
> **H. G. Wells**

This book is dedicated to colloquial speakers of English across the globe. Fellow speakers, take issue with those who say that the English language is in decline; turn away from those who foresee its destruction; do not be bogged down in the slough of despondent grammar books; enter not the valley of humiliating purists; and neither spend too long in the vain pursuit of fair English, nor in doubting one's own words. Trample on over the path of righteous critics, and enter not into conversation with Mr Wordy Wiseman. Above all be not timorous of holding forth in one's own tongue. Though the path to good writing and speaking be beset by pitfalls, remember, you do not walk it alone.

Antal Parody
(with apologies to John Bunyan – a master of the
colloquial English of his time)

TERMS OF REFERENCE

EAT, to put in the mouth, chew and swallow
i.e. *to eat one's words*.

SHITE, defecate; excrement
i.e. *to talk shite*.

LEAVE, go away from
i.e. *leaves standard English;* leaves behind
i.e. *leaves behind a stinking pile of* ... let's leave it at that.

CRAP, faeces; chaff; refuse from fat-boiling; nonsense
i.e. *that's a load of crap*.

ENGLISH, the language invented by the people of England,
which is used and abused throughout the world
i.e. *I speak the English good, no*?

INTRODUCTION

Ever since man sought to express himself in the English language, there has always been somebody else telling him he has been using it incorrectly. But, in spite of this, English survived, put down its roots, grew its shoots and flourished, and there are now more users of English as a first or second language in the world than any other. English is certainly well used, but does it matter if it is not used well?

The English language has always been at the mercy of those who attempt to impose law and order upon it; to mould its shape, to harness it and prevent it from running off down a wrong path. But English is an unruly animal. Seeking to tame it or preserve its pedigree is a futile task; to use a well-worn phrase, it's like shutting the stable door after the horse has bolted.

To put it another way, if you make language static and deprive it of sustenance, it gets thin and weak and dies. To keep a language going it has to keep growing, and if like most of today's children it has a preference for junk food over meat and two veg, should we starve it?

'Stop right there!' thunder the strict grammarians, citing elegance, clarity, economy of expression, and careful writing, which are found in what is known as standard English, the Queen's English, BBC English and the educated English of the higher echelons of British society. Allow colloquial barbarisms, licentious idioms, dreadful jargon, pretentious vulgarisms, sullied syntax and worse? 'Never!' say the language snobs.

So what about the rest of us? The language slobs? Well, English doesn't have to be stuffy, dry, dull and dreary, corseted and repressed. English can be bent and twisted, played and toyed with, invented and reinterpreted.

Be wary, for today's shite may well be tomorrow's mouthful. In the words of Horace (whose language *did* die), 'Many terms which have now dropped out of favour will be revived, and those that are at present respectable will drop out, if usage so choose . . .'

So let's not allow English to dry up. Let's keep it flowing freely and avoid constipation. That's why this book is about crap – crap English, that is – and how to use it.

THE COMPLETE RULES OF GOOD WRITING (1)

To help avoid any misunderstanding about the scope of this book, it would be as well to pay close attention to the following rules.

A writer should not annoy half of his readers by using gender-specific language.

Always finish what you star

Avoid overuse of ampersands & abbreviations, etc.

Analogies in writing are like feathers on a snake.

Always avoid annoying alliteration.

Avoid trendy locutions that sound flaky.

Always pick on the correct idiom.

A writer must not shift your point of view.

Avoid clichés like the plague – they're so old hat.

Be more-or-less specific.

Consult the dictonary frequently to avoid mispeling.

Comparisons are as bad as clichés.

Contractions aren't necessary.

> 'Easy reading is damned hard writing.'
> **Nathaniel Hawthorne**

TEN EXAMPLES OF CRAP ENGLISH

A comma here and a hyphen there would make all the difference to these needlessly misleading sentences.

1. Waitresses required for breakfast.
2. The box contained old Enid Blytons sex books and videos.
3. She liked cooking Delia Smith in particular.
4. He put on his dress shirt and shoes.
5. Slow workmen in road.
6. I decided on an alteration of course.
7. Elephants please stay in your car.
8. Playground fine for littering.
9. The man who hunts ducks out on weekends.
10. Monster man eating shark.

WORDS' WORTH: TEN HIGHLY INACCURATE WORDS

1. boxing ring – the playing area is square, not round.
2. eggplant – there is no egg in eggplant.
3. hamburger – there is no ham in hamburger.
4. hot dog – there is no dog [one hopes] in this frankfurter sausage inserted in a bread roll.
5. quicksand – this is sand in which one sinks slowly.
6. pineapple – there is neither apple nor pine in pineapple.
7. sweetmeats – there is no meat in these.
8. sweetbreads – there is neither bread nor sweetness in these meats.
9. English muffins – these were not invented in England.
10. French fries – these were not invented in France.

NO WONDER CHILDREN AREN'T LEARNING GOOD ENGLISH IF THEY FOLLOW THESE EXAMPLES

'Why not have the kids shot for Easter, or have a
family portrait taken?
What have you got to lose?'

'Dinner Special: Turkey £2.35; Chicken or Beef £2.25; Children £2.00.'

'No children aloud.'

'Dog for sale: eats anything and is fond of children.'

'For anyone who has children and doesn't know this, there is a
crèche on the first floor.'

'The older children will be presenting Shakespeare's *Hamlet* in the
church basement on Friday at 7 p.m. The congregation is invited to
attend this tragedy.'

'Scouts are saving cans, bottles, and other items to be recycled.
Proceeds will be used to cripple children.'

THIS TREE IS A SYMBOL
OF OUR MUM.
PEACEFUL, STRONG AND
SHELTERING FROM
HER CHILDREN.

'Children are as interested in books
as they ever are.'
BBC NEWS

THE HALLMARKS OF BAD WRITING: SOME GRAMMATICALLY CORRECT SENTENCES

1. The cotton clothing is usually made from grows in Mississippi.
2. When Fred eats food gets thrown.
3. The horse raced past the barn fell.
4. Prime number few.
5. We painted the wall with cracks.
6. Fat people eat accumulates.
7. Mary gave the child the dog bit a plaster.
8. I convinced her children are noisy.
9. Until the police arrest the drug dealers control the street.
10. The dog that I had really loved bones.

None of these 'garden-path sentences' is actually incorrect or incomplete, but if you find that you're still up the garden path with them, here's how they could also be written:

1. The cotton **that** clothing is usually made from grows in Mississippi.
2. When Fred eats **his dinner** food gets thrown.
3. The horse **which was** raced past the barn, fell **down**.
4. Prime **people** number few.
5. We painted the wall **that was covered** with cracks.
6. **The** fat **that** people eat accumulates **in their bodies**.
7. Mary gave the child **that** the dog bit a plaster.
8. I convinced her **that** children are noisy.
9. Until the police arrest **them**, the drug dealers control the street.
10. The dog **that I had as a pet** really loved bones.

TEN TRULY TRICKY SENTENCES

1. He knows more beautiful women than Miss World.
*Does he know women who are more beautiful than Miss World,
or are a greater number of beautiful women known to him than
are known to Miss World?*

2. I know a man with a wooden leg named Smith.
*You do? Well was the man called Smith, or did the man call his
leg Smith?*

3. She enjoyed painting models nude.
She liked painting nude models or painting in the nude?

4. My daughter has grown another foot.
Three feet? How does she walk?

5. Visiting relatives can be boring.
We know that, but are they coming to us, or are we going to them?

6. Veggies don't know how good meat tastes.
Meat in general, or good meat specifically?

7. I saw the man with the binoculars.
But which of us was using them?

8. He had a smash with a black cab driver.
Was the vehicle or the cab driver black?

9. I want to buy a card and brown paper for her present.
Nice present!

10. We will sell petrol to people in a plastic container.
How do you get in a plastic container?

> 'I once shot an elephant in my pyjamas.
> How he got into my pyjamas I'll never know.'
> **Groucho Marx**

THE COMPLETE RULES OF GOOD WRITING (2)

Do not use, unnecessary, commas.

Do not use a foreign word when there is an adequate English quid pro quo.

Do not use hyperbole; not even one in a million can do it effectively.

Don't repeat yourself and avoid being repetitive.

Don't use no double negatives. The double negative is a no-no.

Don't be redundant; don't use more words than necessary; it's highly superfluous.

Don't indulge in sesquipedalian lexicological constructions.

Don't overuse exclamation marks!!!

Don't repeat yourself, or say again what you have said before.

'Don't use unattributed quotations.'

TEN MORE EXAMPLES OF CRAP ENGLISH

1. She rewed the day she met him.
2. Anti fox killing campaigners.
3. Mixing bowl set designed to please a cook with round bottom for efficient beating.
4. For sale buy owner.
5. Don't run on the stairs use the handrail.
6. Yoko Ono will talk about her husband John Lennon who was killed in an interview with Barbara Walters.
7. Toilet for sitting-down customers only.
8. For sale: a quilted high chair that can be made into a table, potty, rocking horse, refrigerator, spring coat, size 8 and fur collar.
9. Don't let your worries kill you, let the church help.
10. Wanted man to take care of cow that does not smoke or drink.

HOW TO DANGLE YOUR MODIFIERS

A 'dangling modifier' is a phrase or clause that conveys something different from what is intended, which causes the meaning of the sentence to be left 'dangling', as the following examples prove.

An old newspaper sat on the table she had finished with.

She left the novel on the side of the bath which she'd started reading.

I'll type up the minutes for the office staff covered in the meeting.

Walking my dog on the path, laughing loudly.

The car sat in the garage which wouldn't start earlier.

The meal for the children she was cooking.

The man sat on the horse that she had kissed earlier.

He cut the grass with his new mower which was already a foot high.

She slipped on the ice and apparently her legs went in separate directions in early December.

The baby was delivered, the cord clamped and cut, and handed to the paediatrician, who breathed and cried immediately.

WHY ENGLISH IS CRAP (1)

Have you ever asked yourself . . .

Why when the stars are out, they can be seen, but when the lights are out, they cannot be seen?

Why when one gets fit one is healthy, but when one has a fit one is ill?

Why a fast horse runs and fast colours don't?

Why one can ship by truck and send truck by ship?

Why a seeded loaf has seeds in it, but seeded raisins have them taken out?

Why one's house goes up in flames at the same time as it is burning down?

_____

WORD TROUBLE

'It depends on how you define "alone" . . . there were a lot of times when we were alone, but I never really thought we were.'
Bill Clinton

'Rarely is the question asked: is our children learning?'
George W. Bush

'It depends on what the meaning of the word "is" is.'
Bill Clinton

CARPING ON

Do you find it reassuring that doctors call what they do practice?

Why when I wind up my watch do I start it, but when I wind up a project I end it?

Would you rather own a genuine imitation or an authentic replica?

How come overtones and undertones are the same thing?

How do you get off a non-stop flight?

Why isn't phonetic spelled the way it sounds?

Why is it that night falls but day breaks?

If no man is an island, where does that leave the Isle of Man?

'And later we'll go over to Rome, where three paintings
have been stolen by Van Gogh and Cézanne.'
James Proctor

HOW IMPORTANT IS SPELLING?

Interesting fact: Only 17 per cent of native English speakers can spell the following six words correctly: height, necessary, accommodation, separate, sincerely, business.

Interesting fact: English spelling is more complex, irregular and eccentric than that of almost any other written language.

Interesting fact: Due to its spelling practices, English is the hardest European language to learn to read and write.

Interesting fact: Shakespeare's name has been spelled eighty different ways.

SPELLING BEE (1)

How many of the following commonly misspelled words would you be able to spell correctly?

accomodate/accommodate/acommodate	=	accommodate
advocado/avocado/advocardo	=	avocado
allege/alledge/aledge	=	allege
assocation/association/asociation	=	association
believe/beleive/beleeve	=	believe
calender/calandar/calinder	=	calendar
definite/definate/definete	=	definite
diarrhoea/direrear/dihorrea	=	diarrhoea
embarrass/embarass/embaras	=	embarrass
exstasy/ecstasy/ecstacy/extacy	=	ecstasy

ENUFF IS ENUFF!

Did you know that more than one-tenth of English words are not spelled the way they sound? Try the letter combination 'ough' out for size:

A rough-coated, dough-faced, thoughtful ploughman strode through the streets of Scarborough; after falling into a slough, he coughed and hiccoughed.

A basic guide to the pronunciation of each word follows:

rough as in 'puff'
dough as in 'oh'
thoughtful as in 'port'
ploughman as in 'thou'
through as in 'too'

Scarborough as in 'curragh'
slough as in 'buff'
coughed as in 'soft'
hiccoughed as in 'cupped'

CRAP ENGLISH WORDS

arse, babble, baloney, blah blah blah, bosh, bull, bullshit, bum-fodder, bunkum, cobblers, codswallop, crap, crock of shit, double Dutch, drivel, drone, flannel, fustian, gabble, gammon, garbage, gas, gibberish, Greek, guff, hooey, hogwash, hokum, jabberwocky, jargon, jaw, nonsense, piddling, purple, rot, solecism, tosh, twaddle, verbiage, waffle, wind, yackety-yak.

THE TROUBLE WITH SPELLING: SPELLING THE WORD AS IT SOUNDS (1)

accident	–	axident
accommodate	–	akomodate
because	–	becoz
bread	–	bred
chaos	–	kaoss
cough	–	coff
conscious	–	conshuss
cyclist	–	syklist
debt	–	det
delicious	–	delishuss
enough	–	enuff
fastidious	–	fastidius
English	–	Inglish
friend	–	frend
foreigner	–	forener
gauge	–	gage
guarantee	–	garantee

SPELLING SOLUTIONS: SHORTEN THE ALPHABET

What if you decided that the letter 'c' should be dropped from the alphabet and should be replased by either the letter 'k' or 's', and also that the letter 'x' should be removed? The only kase in which 'c' would be retained would be the 'ch' formation.

Then you might decide to reform the use of the letter 'w', so that 'which' and 'one' take the same konsonant, and you might replase 'y' with 'i' and fiks the 'g/j' anomali wonse and for all.

Jenerally, then, the improvement would kontinue iear bi iear bi doing awai with useless double konsonants, and modifiing vowlz and rimeining voist and unvoist konsonants.

It wud finali be posibl tu meik use ov the ridandant letez 'c', 'y' and 'x'; – bi now jast a memori in the mindz ov uold doderez – tu riplais 'ch', 'sh' and 'th' rispektivli.

Finali, xen, afta sum 20 iears ov orxogrefkl riform, wi wud hev a lojikl, kohirent speling in ius xrewawt xe Ingliy-spiking werld.

WHY ENGLISH IS CRAP (2)

Has it ever occurred to you ...

Why feet smell and noses run?

Why one fills in a form by filling out the applicable boxes?

Why homeowners put on alarms and intruders make them go off?

Why a mediocre athlete has a slim chance of getting a medal,
but a fat chance of getting the gold?

Why the human race will not win the race against time?

Why one can recite from a play and play at a recital?

Why one trains on a track and a train runs on tracks?

CARPING ON AGAIN

Why is it you can walk down a road, even if it goes uphill?

Why is the time of day with the slowest traffic called rush hour?

Why do slow down and slow up mean the same thing?

Why do flammable and inflammable mean the same thing?

Why do overlook and oversee mean opposite things?

Why do people sit down during the day and sit up late at night?

Why do caregiver and caretaker mean the same thing?

Why do we say that something is rock solid, meaning immovable, but we rock a cradle?

If money makes the world go around, how come bills travel at twice the speed of cheques?

SPELLING SOLUTIONS: ELIMINATE LONG WORDS (1)

ABSTEMIOUSNESS (14 letters), meaning being sparing in the use of food and strong drink.

DISPROPORTIONABLENESS (21 letters), meaning lack of proportion or unsuitableness to something else. (It appears in the *Guinness Book of Records* as 'the longest word in common use'.)

ESCHATOLOGICAL (14 letters), meaning pertaining to the last or final things.

FLOCCINAUCINIHILIPILIFICATION (29 letters), meaning an estimation of something as worthless. (It is supposedly the longest real word in the English language, according to the *Oxford English Dictionary*.)

GALACTOPHAGOUS (14 letters), meaning feeding on milk.

HONORIFICABILITUDINITATIBUS (27 letters), meaning the state of being able to achieve honours. (This is the longest word used by Shakespeare and appears in *Love's Labour's Lost*, Act V, Scene I.)

INCOMPREHENSIBILITIES (21 letters), qualities of being incomprehensible.

JUXTAPOSITION (13 letters), the position of being side by side or close together.

KALEIDOSCOPICALLY (17 letters), meaning in a kaleidoscopic way.

LIPOGRAMMATISM (14 letters), meaning the art of writing lipograms (a type of writing that omits all words containing a particular letter of the alphabet).

'There are lots of "ifs" in motor racing and "if" is a very long word.'
Murray Walker

> Did you know that the longest word
> in the dictionary is SMILES because there's
> a mile between the two Ss?

THE COMPLETE RULES OF GOOD WRITING (3)

Eliminate quotations. As Ralph Waldo Emerson once said, 'I hate quotations. Tell me what you know.'

Eschew obfuscation.

Employ the vernacular.

Everyone should be careful to use a singular pronoun with singular nouns in their writing.

Exaggeration is a million times worse than understatement.

Go around the barn at high noon to avoid colloquialisms.

Hopefully, you will use words correctly, irregardless of how others use them.

It is wrong to ever split an infinitive.

If you reread and reread your work and reread it again you will weed out the weeds of repetition.

If any word is improper at the end of a sentence, a linking verb is.

It behoves you to avoid archaic expressions.

PREPOSITIONS: THINGS TO FEEL FREE TO END SENTENCES WITH

The idea that ending a sentence with a preposition is wrong is a myth; a fiction, not a rule. Robert Lowth, an eighteenth-century Bishop of London, reputedly started this affectation; he thought it impolite to round one's words off. Indeed, one should round off one's words. Thus we gained, 'The person to whom I must write', rather than 'The person I must write to'; 'The English lecture to which I should go', rather than 'The English lecture I should go to'. However, most people now accept that this is just stuffy pretension and not bad writing.

So, are the following sentences examples of crap English?

> The English teacher whom I must put up with.
> The English teacher with whom I must put up.
>
> The style it is written in.
> The style in which it is written.
>
> Which friends are you going to the concert with?
> With which friends are you going to the concert?
>
> What have you based that story on?
> On what have you based that story?
>
> The pen he drew on the wall with.
> The pen with which he drew on the wall.
>
> I have just run that rabbit over.
> I have just run over that rabbit.
>
> I just tied that dog up.
> I just tied up that dog.
>
> What is she playing at?
> At what is she playing?

TROUBLESOME PREPOSITIONS

'Put food on your family!'
George W. Bush

'It's been every colour under the rainbow.'
Toyah Willcox

'It's unlucky to walk under a black cat.'
Max Kauffmann

'If is a very big preposition.'
John Major

'It's all the language that gets in the way . . . I can't keep my head above the prepositions!'
Jim Carrey

'May I end this sentence with a proposition?'
Chat-up line

'This is the sort of English up with which I will not put.'
Winston Churchill

SPELLING SOLUTIONS: ELIMINATE LONG WORDS (2)

MYELENCEPHALOUS (15 letters), meaning having a brain and spinal cord.

ONOMATOPOEICALLY (16 letters), meaning having the properties of onomatopoeia – a word which imitates a sound e.g. tinkle, hiss, buzz.

PNEUMONOULTRAMICROSCOPICSILICOVOLCANOCONIOSIS (45 letters), a lung disease caused by breathing in certain particles; the longest word in any English-language dictionary, although open to dispute as it is a made-up word.

QUADRAGENARIOUS (15 letters), meaning forty years old.

RHINOTILLEXOMANIA (17 letters), meaning an obsession with nosepicking.

SUPERCALIFRAGILISTICEXPIALIDOCIOUS (34 letters), from the film *Mary Poppins*. Often quoted as the longest word in English, although mistakenly so.

TINTINNABULATION (16 letters), meaning a ringing or tinkling sound, as that made by bells.

UNREASONABLENESS (16 letters), meaning the state of being unreasonable.

VINDICTIVENESS (14 letters), meaning vengefulness.

XANTHOMELANOUS (14 letters), pertaining to races of men with an olive, brown or yellow complexion and black hair.

ZENZIZENZIZENZIC (16 letters), meaning the eighth power of a number.

NEEDLESS TO SAY, MANY WORDS ARE BETTER THAN ONE

Are you tired of succinct sentences, of plain and simple meanings, of clear and direct phrases, of getting to the point? Do you want to make your sentences carry more weight? If you have answered yes to any of the above, then just add words. After all, why use one when so many more are available? The following examples show how you can bulk out your English by replacing perfectly adequate words with the following empty phrases.

because	–	because of the fact that
because	–	due to the fact that
each	–	each individual man/woman/adult/child/boy/ girl/dog/cat/mouse
each	–	each and every single solitary individual man/woman . . .
few	–	a fraction of
few	–	a teeny tiny fractional fraction of
hopefully	–	I am full of hope that
if	–	in the event that
more	–	an increasing proportion of
more	–	a still ever increasing proportion of
most	–	the vast majority of
now	–	at the present time
now	–	at this moment in time
soon	–	in the near future
whether	–	the question as to whether
whether	–	the question as to the question as to whether

'One word sums up probably the responsibility of any Vice President, and that one word is "to be prepared."'
Dan Quayle

ESSENTIAL PADDING

A selection of twenty words and phrases which one can scatter among one's writing and conversation.

apparently
at this point in time
for the most part
generally
I feel that
in a manner of speaking
in order to
in some ways
it is considered very important that

at the same time
for all intents and purposes
for the purpose of
I believe that
I'm glad you asked me that question
in my opinion
in reality
in the region of
it is important to stress that

THE LONG AND THE SHORT OF IT

Verbosity, *n.* the unnecessary use of more words than are actually needed, whether in a piece of written text or in speech.

'Sir, I would hereby draw your esteemed attention to the way my talents are in tandem with your company's long-term goals.' [What not to write in a covering letter to a prospective employer.]

'We are currently in the process of consolidating our product range to ensure that the products that we stock are indicative of our brand aspirations. As part of our range consolidation we have also decided to revisit our supplier list and employ a more intelligent system for stock acquisition. As a result of the above certain product lines are now unavailable, whilst potentially remaining available from more mainstream suppliers.' [Website response to a customer enquiry about whether it sold blank CDs.]

'It is essential, if you hope to maintain a clear and comprehensible writing style, that you always strive to keep your language as plain and unadorned as it is possible to keep it, however hard you may find that to do.' [An education website's example of a verbose sentence which could have been uttered in less than five words.]

LOST FOR WORDS

Basically, like, our daily conversations are quite literally peppered with unnecessary words, y'know, that we automatically use, sort of, when we're trying to think of the right word to describe . . . errr . . . our, like, situation or state of mind.

at the end of the day	basically
y'know	kind of
if you know what I mean	um
do you get me?	like
if you catch my drift	errr
sort of	well
innit?	know what I mean?
sort of thing	um

SPELLING BEE (2)

More tricky words to spell correctly.

February/Febury/Febuary/Feburee	=	February
govenment/government/goverment	=	government
harass/harrass/haras	=	harass
jewelery/jewllry/jewellery	=	jewellery
knowledge/knowladge/knowlidge	=	knowledge
leisure/liesure/lesure	=	leisure
libery/libary/library/libry	=	library
milennium/millennium/millenium	=	millennium
necessary/necesary/neccessary	=	necessary
occasionally/ocasionally/ocassionly	=	occasionally
occurrence/occurrance/ocurence	=	occurrence

FUSTIAN FLANNEL

'Verbosity leads to unclear, inarticulate things.'
Dan Quayle

'Reports that say that something hasn't happened are always
interesting to me, because as we know, there are known knowns;
there are things we know we know. We also know there are known
unknowns; that is to say we know there are some things we do not
know. But there are also unknown unknowns – the ones we don't
know we don't know.'
Donald Rumsfeld

'Hawaii has always been a very pivotal role in the Pacific. It is
in the Pacific. It is a part of the United States that is an island
that is right here.'
Dan Quayle

'I think that [the film] *Clueless* was very deep. I think it was deep in
the way that it was very light. I think lightness has to come from a
very deep place if it's true lightness.'
Alicia Silverstone

'What a waste it is to lose one's mind. Or not to have a mind is being
very wasteful. How true that is.'
Dan Quayle

MORE ESSENTIAL PADDING

I think that
literally
needless to say
one tends to
studies have found that
there is no escaping the fact that
various
virtually

it would seem that
moreover
on consideration
really
the vast majority of
until such time as
very
with the possible exception of

THE TROUBLE WITH SPELLING:
SPELLING THE WORD AS IT SOUNDS (2)

height	–	hite
honour	–	onerr
knowledge	–	nollege
language	–	langwidge
light	–	lite
people	–	peeple
photo	–	foto
recommend	–	rekomend
says	–	sez
said	–	sed
see	–	C
slight	–	slite
success	–	sucksess
through	–	thru
tough	–	tuff
unconsious	–	unconshus
upright	–	uprite
view	–	vyew
weight	–	wate
when	–	wen
writing	–	riting
yacht	–	yot
you	–	U

THE COMPLETE RULES OF GOOD WRITING (4)

It is recommended that measures should be taken to ensure that the length of sentences is not excessive and that the complexity of said sentences is reduced.

Never use a big word where a diminutive alternative would suffice.

No sentence fragments.

Never use two words where a single expression will do.

One should never generalize.

One-word sentences? Eliminate. Always!

Parenthetical marks, however relevant, are unnecessary.

Parenthetical words like these should be enclosed in commas.

Proofread carefully to see if you any words out.

Place pronouns as close as possible, especially in long sentences, as of ten or more words, to their antecedents.

Placing a comma between subject and predicate, is not correct.

Prepositions are not words to end sentences with.

STUFFY AND ANTIQUATED WORDS BEGINNING WITH 'WHERE'

whereat
wherefore
whereinto
whereso'er
whereto
whereupon

whereby
wherefrom
whereof
wheresoever
whereuntil
wherewith

where'er
wherein
whereout
wherethrough
whereunto
wherewithal

THE COLOUR PURPLE

Sometimes, we can get carried away with the use of overelaborate wordage in an effort to appear intellectual, knowledgeable and perhaps a cut above the rest. Anyway, here's some simple words made plummier, for those who enjoy a spot of purple prose and excessively ornate writing.

aware – cognizant
buy – purchase
different – disparate
drunk – inebriated
group – assembly
name – appellation
rude – impertinent
shorten – abbreviate
talk – communicate
use – utilize

bad-tempered – cantankerous
decorating – interior design
doctor – physician
eat – consume
lowest – bottommost
noisy – cacophonous
secret – clandestine
small – infinitesimal
teacher – educator
weatherman – meteorologist

> 'Frequently with serious works and ones of great import, some purple patch or other is stitched on, to show up far and wide.'
> **Horace**

MORE FUSTIAN FLANNEL

'I know that you believe that you understood what you think
I said, but I am not sure you realize that what you heard is not
what I meant.'
Robert McCloskey, US State Department spokesman

'The theories – the ideas she expressed about equality of results
within legislative bodies and with – by outcome, by decisions
made by legislative bodies, ideas related to proportional voting as
a general remedy, not in particular cases where the circumstances
make that a feasible idea . . .'
Al Gore

'My friends, no matter how rough the road may be, we can and
we will, never, never surrender to what is right.'
Dan Quayle

'A sophistical rhetorician, inebriated with the exuberance of his
own verbosity, and gifted with an egotistical imagination that
can at all times command an interminable and inconsistent
series of arguments to malign an opponent and to
glorify himself.'
Benjamin Disraeli (about William Gladstone)

'He draweth out the thread of his verbosity finer than
the staple of his argument.'
William Shakespeare, *Love's Labour's Lost*

G'BYE TO ALL THAT: WHY CLIPPED FORMS SAVE STUFFINESS

Saying things the long way, in their complete and fullest forms, isn't always the best way. Getting to the point is often so much better.

As my automobile was still in the garage, I telephoned the omnibus company to see if the omnibuses were running on time. I decided that it would be quicker to travel to the gymnasium by bicycle. However, as it was so cold I worried that my cough might turn into influenza. I had intended to buy some comestibles on the way home, but I had enough food in the refrigerator as it turned out. I decided to go to bed and watch a television programme, of which I am a fanatic, but the aeroplanes overhead kept drowning out the sound.

NEEDLESS INFORMATION GIVEN TO CONSUMERS

Product will be hot after heating. [on a microwaveable meal]

Do not use while sleeping. [on a hairdryer]

Wearing this garment does not enable you to fly.
[supplied with a Superman costume]

Open packet, eat nuts. [on a packet of nuts, served during a flight]

After opening, keep upright. [on a carton of milk]

Paint-Stripper Heat Gun: NOT TO BE USED AS A HAIRDRYER.
[on a paint-stripper heat gun, needless to say]

TAUTOLOGIES AND PLEONASMS (1)

Tautology, *n.* the saying of the same thing twice over using different words, i.e. needless repetition of words expressing the same idea; sameness of expression which adds nothing either to the sense or the rhetorical effect; redundancy of words in speaking or writing.

Pleonasm, *n.* the use of more words than are necessary to convey a particular meaning, i.e. needless repetition of words expressing the same idea; sameness of expression which adds nothing either to the sense or the rhetorical effect; redundancy of words in speaking or writing.

completely decimated
minute detail
absolute truth
closet claustrophobic
really unreal
blue in colour
close scrutiny
fatally slain
basic essentials
razed to the ground
8 p.m. in the evening
uniquely original
verbally tell
personally see
I saw it with my own eyes

almost unique
absolutely equal
future plans
incredibly believable
square in shape
end result
absolutely final
completely exhausted
true facts
4 a.m. in the morning
penniless pauper
visually see
physically search
freezing ice
false lie

'What I tell you three
times is true.'
Lewis Carroll,
The Hunting of the Snark

DODGY DIALECTS:
YORKSHIRE YAMMER

Regional variations in the English language may be regarded as a challenge to both ear and mind. While various dialects may be fascinating, to the outsider it can sometimes be impossible to make any sense of the curious pronunciations and alternative vocabulary used to converse in different parts of the country.

an'all – as well/also	any road – anyway
aye – yes	awlus – always
brass – money	bray – beat/hit
gie'o'er – stop it	'appen – perhaps
in't'it? – isn't it?	jiggered – tired
mardy – moody	mash – brew
missell – myself	missen – myself
mither – harass	mucky – dirty
nivver – never	ommast – almost
neet – night	nobbut – only
nowt – nothing	parky – chilly
reyt – right/very	summat – something
sup – drink	tha/thee – you
think on – remember	wi'owt – without
ye'sell – yourself	ye'sen – yourself

43

SUPERFLUOUS TO SAY: CELEBRITY STYLE (1)

'And that's a self-portrait of himself, by himself.'
Richard Madeley

'Now we go into lap fifty-three, the penultimate last lap but one.'
Murray Walker

'It looks like being a busy weekend on the ferries, particularly
Saturday and Sunday.'
Peter Powell

'It was a sudden and unexpected surprise.'
BBC Old Bailey correspondent

'I made a wrong mistake.'
Yogi Berra

'I never make predictions, especially about the future.'
Samuel Goldwyn

'Every rugby international is totally unique – and this one
is just the same.'
England rugby player

'I always used to go for blondes and quiet girls, but Victoria is
the total opposite – dark and loud.'
David Beckham

'I've said I've never broken the drug laws of my country,
and that is the absolute truth.'
Bill Clinton

'It's déjà vu all over again.'
Yogi Berra

EXCUSE ME, YOU JUST SAID THAT: EXAMPLES OF UNNECESSARY REPETITION

When people want what they are saying to carry that extra bit of weight they add unnecessary words – 'repetitive redundancies' as they are sometimes described. Here are some examples of where less would equal more.

'So it's Mexico, Mexico, Mexico. Speaking of Mexico, here's a piece from Brazil.'
Henry Kelly

'I'd love it if we beat them, I'd love it.'
Kevin Keegan

'At least it was a victory and at least we won.'
Bobby Moore

'I'm not disappointed – just disappointed.'
Kevin Keegan

'I'm the king of the world, I am the greatest, I'm Muhammad Ali, I shook up the world, I am the greatest, I'm king of the world, I'm pretty, I'm pretty, I'm a baaaad man, you heard me I'm a baaad man, Archie Moore fell in four, Liston wanted me more, so since he's so great, I'm a gonna make him fall in eight, I'm a baaad man, I'm king of the world! I'm twenty-two years old and ain't gotta mark on my face, I'm pretty, I easily survived six rounds with that ugly bear, because I am the greatest.'
Muhammad Ali

'If one doctor doctors another doctor, does the doctor who doctors the doctor doctor the doctor the way the doctor he is doctoring doctors? Or does he doctor the doctor the way the doctor who doctors doctors?'
Anonymous

SAY THAT AGAIN:
TEN HEALTHY REPETITIONS

It can be hard work thinking up different words. So why do it unless it's really necessary?

1. I spent last evening evening out a pile of papers.

2. Since there is no time like the present, why don't we present the present.

3. The bandage was wound around the wound.

4. The dump was so full that it had to refuse more refuse.

5. Your invalid insurance is invalid.

6. The patient will have to be patient and wait patiently.

7. A sewer doing her sewing fell down a sewer.

8. After a number of injections, my arm got number.

9. He could lead if he would get the lead out.

10. The farm was used to produce produce.

TAUTOLOGIES AND PLEONASMS (2)

tautological pleonasms
brilliant genius
known unknowns
free gift
adequate enough
revert back
very particular
usual custom
close proximity
final conclusion
a new innovation
short in length
surrounded on all sides
arguably unarguable
exactly the same

pleonastic tautologies
known knowns
necessary essentials
hollow tunnel
an added bonus
very widespread
I heard it with my own ears
personal opinion
reason why
final completion
small in size
huge giant
temporary break
a total of 100 people
lonely isolation

ALREADY DONE: WORDS BEGINNING WITH 'AFORE'

afore
aforecited
aforegoing
aforehand
aforementioned

aforenamed
aforesaid
aforethought
aforetime

Unnecessary warning on
a nuclear warhead

DO NOT DROP

THE DOUBLE NEGATIVE: NO NO OR DON'T KNOW?

The double negative is a repetition of the sign of negation and is regarded as sub-standard English when there is no intention of having the two negatives cancel each other out. In other words, it doesn't do nothing for language. However, even those who pride themselves on speaking standard English are sometimes caught out by a no no.

You aren't but human.

He can't make friends with no one.

She isn't but a homeless child.

I've so much to do that I haven't never got the time to sit down any more.

She doesn't never eat since she's been on that diet.

They didn't have no apples.

I never saw nobody.

They didn't know nothing.

My children don't never visit me now that they have left home.

She hadn't never been so tired.

I couldn't travel nowhere by aeroplane.

He hasn't been married not a month.

He knew his clothing wouldn't be no protection from the winter weather.

I am not going to buy no car.

She never went nowhere yesterday.

The boy didn't have no bicycle.

Incidentally, is 'can can' a double positive?

SUPERFLUOUS TO SAY: CELEBRITY STYLE (2)

' . . . and he would stand there staring at him with his eyes.'
BBC Commentator

'We've been asked to do *Playboy* together, me and Victoria, as a pair.'
David Beckham

'They've written their own number – it's an original number and it's written by themselves.'
Jenny Lee-Wright

'So the VAT increase on a second-hand car is just another added addition.'
Adrian Love

'With a couple of minutes to go he had scored two goals in a two-minute period.'
Alan Perry

'The answer's an affirmative "yes".'
Nigel Mansell

'I am speaking from a deserted and virtually empty Crucible Theatre.'
David Vine

'I don't normally do requests, unless I'm asked to.'
Richard Whiteley

'And Watford acknowledge the support of the crowd, indeed of the crowd that supported them.'
Barry Davies

'You can't compare two players who are different because they're not the same.'
Glenn Hoddle

NEEDLESS TO SAY, LIKE: HIDDEN EXTRAS

Being as how it was him, like.
He was all over me, like, you know what I mean.
I got it off of the table and put it up on the shelf.
They didn't hardly have enough food left.
He speaks better English than what people realize.
I was disappointed because I couldn't go neither.
I'm not saying that I didn't like it, like, know what I mean?
They don't never visit us, like.
I can't hardly wait to get off of this bus.

Worrying warning on a
nuclear warhead

DO NOT NOT DROP

WRITE IT LONG, WRITE IT LARGE

An acceptable sentence length is between 17 and 24 words.
Sentences over 40 words are rarely effective.
A grammarian

Curse the blasted, jelly-boned swines, the slimy, the belly-wriggling
invertebrates, the miserable soddingrotters, the flaming sods, the
snivelling, dribbling, dithering, palsied, pulse-less lot that make up
England today. [28 words]
D. H. Lawrence

An author ought to consider himself not as a gentleman who gives a
private or eleemosynary treat, but rather as one who keeps a public
ordinary at which all persons are welcome for their money.
[35 words]
Henry Fielding

That young girl is one of the least benightedly unintelligent organic
life forms it has been my profound lack of pleasure not to be able to
avoid meeting. [28 words]
Douglas Adams

But there was something different also, something for which, while
her cheek received the prodigious kiss, she had her opportunity – the
sight of the others, who, having risen from their cards to join the
absent members of their party, had reached the open door at the end
of the room and stopped short, evidently, in presence of the
demonstration that awaited them. [62 words]
Henry James

She plunged into a sea of platitudes, and with the powerful
breaststroke of a channel swimmer, made her confident way towards
the white cliffs of the obvious. [27 words]
W. Somerset Maugham

Did you know? The longest sentence in English literature is spoken
by Molly Bloom, a character in the celebrated novel *Ulysses* by James
Joyce. Containing 4,391 words, this sentence is so long that in the
first edition of the work it extended for more than forty pages.

DODGY DIALECTS: SCOUSE SPEAK

These are just a few of the unique words and phrases which can be heard on the streets of Liverpool.

arlarse – not nice
bizzies – police
cabbaged – confused
creased – tired
dekko – a look
giz – give me
jib it – leave it
la – boy/young man
marmalize – beat up
nimps – easy
owldies – old people
parro – paranoid
rollies – roll-up cigarettes
sparkied – knocked out
webs – feet

avvy – afternoon
bifter – cigarette
come ed! – come on!
deffo – definitely
fire bobbies – fire brigade
grid – face
kidder – friend/brother
leckie – electricity
muzzy – moustache
nix – nothing
ozzie – hospital
plazzie – plastic/fake
sack – stop
trabs – sports shoes
yerwha'? – pardon?

THE COMPLETE RULES OF GOOD WRITING (5)

Refrain from being indirect.
Subject and verb always has to agree.
The recommendation is for the use of verbs rather than nouns.
Take the bull by the hand and avoid mixed metaphors.
The passive voice is to be ignored and should not be used.
Understatement is always the best by far.
Use the apostrophe in it's proper place and omit it when its not needed.
Use youre spell chekker to avoid mispelling and to catch typograhpical errers; they always get it write.
When dangling, watch your participles.
Who needs rhetorical questions?

EXCESS WIND

Most people like to chat, but some of us are just too gassy.

to bang on
to beat one's chops
to chew the rag
to drone on
to have a big gob
to have a gabfest
to have verbal diarrhoea
to go off on one
to lay it on thick
to run off at the mouth
to talk a blue streak
to talk crap

to be an old windbag
to bend one's ear
to chinwag
to flap at the jibs
to have a bull sesh
to have a mouth on her/him
to go on about it
to jawbone
to pile it on
to swallow the dictionary
to talk a lot of hot air
to talk the hind legs off a donkey

NO NEED TO SPELL IT OUT

Grammarians may say that contractions aren't necessary and shoudn't be used in formal writing, but sometimes we need to take short cuts. That's why crap English is for real, busy people, who think life is too short to spell it out every time. Of course, contractions aren't really crap unless you don't know how to use an apostrophe, the little elevated comma thing that fills the gap where a letter or letters have been omitted (Please take note, Mr Shaw). Those favouring such examples as havnt and dont, or ha'vnt and d'ont, should stick to writing their words in full.

aren't	can't
couldn't	daren't
doesn't	don't
hadn't	hasn't
isn't	it's
mightn't	mustn't
needn't	oughtn't
shan't	shouldn't
wasn't	weren't
won't	wouldn't

SPELLING BEE (3)

How would you spell the following words?

pastime/pasttime/past time	=	pastime
prounciation/pronounciation/pronunciation	=	pronunciation
questionaire/questionnaire/questionair	=	questionnaire
rhthym/rhythm/rythm	=	rhythm (rejoice heartily your teacher has measles)
scissors/sissers/sissors	=	scissors
separate/separate/seprate/sepret	=	separate
twelfth/twellfth/twefth	=	twelfth
unntil/untill/until	=	until
vaccum/vacuum/vacume	=	vacuum
weird/wierd/wered	=	weird

'The English have no respect for their language, and will not teach their children to speak it. They spell it so abominably that no man can teach himself what it sounds like.'
George Bernard Shaw, *Pygmalion*

SAY THAT AGAIN: TEN MORE HEALTHY REPETITIONS

1. How can I intimate this to my most intimate friend?

2. I object to that object.

3. I had to subject the subject to a series of subjective tests.

4. The wind was too strong to wind the sail.

5. There was a row between Oxford and Cambridge about how to row.

6. She wasn't close enough to the window to close it.

7. A farmer taught a sow to sow.

8. Upon seeing the tear in my dress, I shed a tear.

9. Polish cleaners polish well.

10. After tying his mistress's bow, the servant gave a courteous bow.

'The cook was a good cook, as cooks go;
and as cooks go, she went.'
Saki (H. H. Munro)

ACRONYMS AND INITIALISMS FOR DAILY USE

An acronym is a word formed from the initial letter of a group of connected words e.g. AIDS, ERNIE, and is pronounced as a word, while an initialism is an abbreviation containing initial letters that are pronounced separately e.g. RAC, BBC. As we are all busy people, surely it makes sense to save our precious time using a little code here and there.

AF	*Archers* fanatic
BP	beautiful people
BTDTGTTS	been there, done that, got the T-shirt
BYOB	bring your own beer
COL	cost of living
DDD	decisions, decisions, decisions
D&I	drunk and incapable
DINKY	double income, no kids yet
EE	*EastEnders*
F&C	fish and chips
GSOH	good salary, own home / good sense of humour
HH	happy hour
KUWTJ	keeping up with the Joneses
LOP	last orders
LOTJ	law of the jungle
LOTL	lie of the land
MTM	married to mogul
NIMBY	not in my back yard
NQR	not quite right
POD	party on, dude
SITCOM	single income, two children, oppressive mortgage

> 'In this age, which believes that there is a short cut to everything, the greatest lesson to be learned is that the most difficult way is, in the long run, the easiest.'
> **Henry Miller**

ACRONYMS AND INITIALISMS FOR LOVERS

AB	ample bosom
ATOU	always thinking of you
BURMA	be undressed, ready, my angel
BOLTOP	better on lips than on paper
EGYPT	ever grasping your pretty tits
FEAR	forget everything and run
FYEO	for your eyes only
GAL	get a life
GTASW	goodbye, that's all she wrote
HAKxx	hugs and kisses
HAQT	he's a cutie
HOHIL	head over heels in love
IAN	in all night
JGF	just good friends
KISS	keep it simple, stupid
KIT	keep in touch

ACRONYMS AND INITIALISMS FOR THE WORKPLACE

AIDA	attention, interest, desire, action
AFK	away from keyboard
AOB	any other business
BAFO	best and final offer
BAU	business as usual
BIBOYS	boss is back on your site
BL	bad lunch
BO	burn out
BOGOF	buy one get one free
BRET	best result every time
CBA	cost-benefit analysis / can't be arsed
CF	cash flow / clever fellow
CGTSTD	can't get the staff these days
CURA	cover your arse
CV	curriculum vitae / computer virus
DED	dog eat dog
DSTM	don't shoot the messenger
FAB	features, advantages, benefits
FIFO	first in, first out
FISH	first in, still here

ENGLISH, YOUR NUMBER'S UP: E-NEOLOGISMS

1nce – once	1stly – firstly	1sty – thirsty
2dA – today	2moro – tomorrow	2nlte – tonight
3dom – freedom	3sm – threesome	4ce – force
4fit – forfeit	4gt – forget	4m – form
4NK8 – fornicate	4t – fought	4tnlt – fortnight
4eva – forever	8 – ate	B13 – baker's dozen

TUMA: TOTALLY UNNECESSARY MEDICAL ABBREVIATIONS (1)

Members of the medical profession are very busy people indeed, so a handy shortcut can save them valuable time when writing a medical report. Doctors and consultants also like to think that they speak a language apart; it would not do for them to have graduated from medical school still speaking the vernacular of the humble patient.

AITM	all in the mind
AMA	against medical advice
AOB	alcohol on breath
AWACBE	as well as can be expected
BTH&H	boogying towards health and happiness
BWS	beached-whale syndrome
CBOH	clean bill of health
CHAOS	chief has arrived on scene
CHUR	see how you are
CTD	close to death/circling the drain
DO	doctor's orders
DOA	dead on arrival/drunk on arrival
DOD	date of death

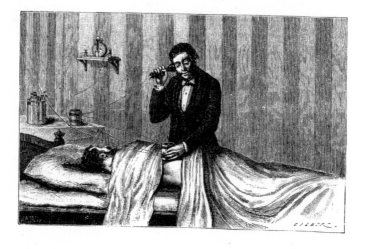

GETTING SHORT: ABBREVIATIONS

Prof. Proper would argue that, in the main, it is poor style to use abbrevs. in writing. On the other hand, abbrevs. make it possible to tell it how it is without fuss or flannel, which is clearly shown in this short e.g.:

b. 1901, d. 1945

It doesn't get much more succinct than that.

MORE ACRONYMS AND INITIALISMS FOR LOVERS

KOTL	kiss on the lips
LDR	long-distance relationship
MUSM	miss you so much
NORWICH	nickers off ready when I come home
PAW	parents are watching
ROR	relationship on rocks
RUU4IT?	are you up for it?
STR	short-term relationship
SWALK	sealed with a loving kiss
TIME	tears in my eyes
TITS	too inebriated to shag
TOPCA	till our paths cross again
TOY	thinking of you
WOS	waste of space
WYSIWYG	what you see is what you get
XM	kiss me
YOYO	you're on your own

MORE ACRONYMS AND INITIALISMS FOR THE WORKPLACE

FYO	for your information
GAFIA	get away from it all
IIARM?	is it a resigning matter?
KMA$	kiss my arse
MBWA	management by wandering around
NB2D	nothing better to do
NOYB	none of your business
PICNIC	problem in chair, not in computer
POETSDAY	piss off early, tomorrow's Saturday
PUOSU	put up or shut up
RTFM	read the fucking manual
SNAFU	situation normal, all fucked up
TGIF	thank God it's Friday
TISWAS	today is Saturday, wear a smile
TMINET	too much information, not enough time
TPTP	the phrase that pays
URUR	you are under review
WFH	working from home
WRS	work-related stress

> **Question:**
> Is the decline of the
> English language due to
> ignorance or apathy?
>
> **Answer:**
> Don't know. Don't care.

TUMA: TOTALLY UNNECESSARY MEDICAL ABBREVIATIONS (2)

ED	effective dose
ENT	ear, nose and throat
FLK	funny-looking kid
GOK	God only knows
HSP	heart-sink patient
INAD	in no acute distress
LOBNAH	lights on, but nobody's at home
MFC	measure for coffin
NDE	near-death experience
PAFO	pissed and fell over
PITA	pain in the arse
SOB	short of breath
TLC	tender loving care
TRO	time ran out
TUBE	totally unnecessary breast examination
WNL	we never looked
WTGP	wants to go private

E-INITIALISMS

B@TM	busy at the moment
CSG	chuckle, snicker, grin
CWUL	chat with you later
DLG	devilish little grin
FDROTFL	falling down, rolling on the floor laughing
GTG	got to go
GTRM	going to read mail
HHOJ	ha, ha, only joking
IABS	I am being sarcastic
L@TO	late at the office
NIFOC	naked in front of computer
OLR	online relationship
O2L	out to lunch
TIC	tongue in cheek
TTFN	ta ta for now
WUWH	wish you were here
VH	virtual hug
VX	virtual kiss

EXPLAIN THYSELF

It's time to face up to the true sense behind some of the things we say, but don't actually mean.

all things considered	I've just come up with this
allegedly	what I am saying is true, but I don't want to be sued
apparently	I've just heard an urban myth
basically	this is going to get complicated
coincidentally	my story is unoriginal
essentially	unimportantly

SUPERFLUOUS TO SAY:
CELEBRITY STYLE (3)

'The robbery was committed by a pair of identical twins.
Both are said to be aged about twenty.'
Paul Hollingsworth

'The margin is very marginal.'
Bobby Robson

'My father was a miner and he worked down a mine.'
Kevin Keegan

'If England lose, they'll be the losers.'
Bob Willis

'I think we agree, the past is over.'
George W. Bush

'He's not going to produce a winner but if he produces second
it'll be the next best thing.'
Murray Walker

'If we do not succeed, we run the risk of failure.'
Dan Quayle

'Sometimes you can observe a lot just by watching.'
Yogi Berra

'With half the race gone, there is half the race still to go.'
Murray Walker

'It was a good match, which could
have gone either way, and very nearly did.'
Jim Sherwin

EUPHEMISTICALLY SPEAKING: AN A-TO-Z OF 'DEAD' TASTELESS EUPHEMISMS

English can be a darned offensive language. Indeed there are some words we just do not like to say, such as bugger, dead or diarrhoea. Neither can we refer to people as bald, fat, short, thick or ugly these days. So thank goodness for euphemisms: acceptable alternatives, inoffensive substitutes, sensitive stand-ins. Or maybe not?

Awaking to life immortal
Basting the formaldehyde turkey
Cooling to room temperature
Dangling in the sheriff's picture frame
(The) Eternal yawn
Feeding the fish
Going into the fertilizer business
Having a reservation at Château Eternity
Immortally challenged
Just add maggots
Kicked the oxygen habit
Left the building
Moved into upper management
Never-ending trip
On the highway express
Permanently out of print
Remaindered
Sent to the dirt archives
Taking an earth bath
Unlicensed on Earth
Visiting time just ended
Went off-line
Zimmer For Sale

CAUGHT SHORT: TWELVE EUPHEMISMS FOR ANSWERING THE CALL OF NATURE

1. Off to chase a rabbit
2. Gone to lay some cable
3. Gone to post a letter
4. Gone to change the barrel
5. Need to make a pit stop
6. Gone to pick daisies
7. Just going to check on the scones
8. Just off to ride the porcelain bus
9. Off to visit St John
10. Gone to explore the geography of the house
11. Gone to powder one's nose
12. Off to spend a penny

COLLYWOBBLES: TWELVE EUPHEMISMS FOR A DODGY TUMMY

1. To do an apple-blossom two-step
2. To do the Aztec hop
3. To have a Delhi belly
4. To have the Edgar Britts
5. To have a gyppy tummy
6. To do the green-apple quickstep
7. To do a Mexican foxtrot
8. To suffer Montezuma's revenge
9. To dance the Patagonian paso doble
10. To ride the porcelain Honda
11. To have the Rangoon runs
12. To have a Singapore tummy

NUDGE NUDGE, WINK WINK: TWENTY EUPHEMISMS FOR SEX

1. Adam and Eve it
2. Bedroom athletics
3. Bump and grind
4. Dance the matrimonial polka
5. Deed, The
6. Fit end to end
7. Fix the plumbing
8. Four-legged frolic
9. Hanky panky
10. Horizontal jogging
11. How's your father
12. Humpty dumpty
13. Knock boots
14. Making babies
15. Making whoopee
16. Nookie
17. Parallel park
18. Quickie
19. Roll in the hay
20. Slap 'n' tickle

EUPHEMISMS FOR BEING A LITTLE CRAZY

A letter short of a word
Not the sharpest pencil in the case
The light's on, but nobody's home
Nutty as a fruit cake
Edited to nothing
A sandwich short of a picnic

A word short of a sentence
Some pages missing
Permanently out to lunch
All ink, no pen
Not all there
Knitting with only one needle

A SMALL SELECTION OF EUPHEMISMS FOR THE PENIS

(N.B. Men have found it necessary to think up hundreds of these!)

Bat and balls	Best leg of three	Chief of staff
Cupid's arrow	Doodle-dandy	Early riser
Excalibur	Family jewels	German soldier
Homo Erectus	John Thomas	Man's best friend
Optimus prime	Percy	Pied Piper
Prince Charming	Rumpleforeskin	Staff of life
Tent pole	Thumper	Todger
Tree of life	Trouser snake	Upright citizen
Viagra baby	Wedding tackle	Willy Winky

POLITICALLY CORRECT EUPHEMISMS

Vertically challenged (short)
Horizontally challenged (fat)
Follically challenged (bald)
Physically challenged (ugly)
Intellectually challenged (thick)
Numerically challenged (innumerate)
Alphabetically challenged (illiterate)
Aurally challenged (deaf)
Verbally challenged (most English speakers)

Getting A Lewinsky

After ex-President Bill Clinton's affair with Monica Lewinsky was exposed, one of NBC's primetime programmes used the term 'getting a Lewinsky' to refer to oral sex. Lewinsky's father promptly lodged a formal complaint. According to *Saturday Night Live* anchor Colin Quinn, NBC's alleged reply to Mr Lewinsky was 'to go "George Michael" himself'.

ROLL OUT THE RHYMING SLANG

Rhyming slang is a colloquial form of English that originated in the last century in London's East End, so that dodgy geezers could conduct their business right under the noses of the local bobbies. (Slang, incidentally, derives from a non-English word *slengjenamn*, meaning nickname.)

Modern rhyming slang is often used euphemistically. Many language enthusiasts appreciate the wit and ingenuity of its specialized vocabulary; on the other hand, there are those who think it pen and inks.

apples (and pears)	stairs
Adam and Eve	believe
boracic (lint)	skint
brown bread	dead
china (plate)	mate (friend)
dog and bone	telephone
Dutch pegs	legs
half-inch	pinch (steal)
Joanna	piano
life and death	breath
mince pies	eyes
pen and ink	stink
plates (of meat)	feet
rub a dub	pub
Ruby (Murray)	curry
syrup (of figs)	wig
tea leaf	thief
two and eight	nervous state
trouble and strife	wife
whistle (and flute)	suit

RUDE RHYMING SLANG

apple tart	fart
bubble gum	bum
Clark Kent	bent
Douglas Hurd	turd
Elephant and Castle	arsehole
fleas and ants	pants
hit and miss	piss
Melvyn Bragg	shag
merchant banker	wanker
Moby Dick	sick
Niagara Falls	balls
Orphan Annie	fanny
Raquel Welch	belch
threepenny bits	tits
two-bob bit	shit

DODGY DIALECTS: SCOTTISH TALK

A selection of words common to many Scots.

ane – one, an		awa – away	
aye – yes		bairn – child	
beastie – animal		bonnie – beautiful/pretty	
braw – handsome/fine		dinnae – don't	
dram – alcoholic drink		dreich – bad (weather)	
fash – trouble/worry		gey – very	
gie – give		guidman – husband	
guidwoman – wife		ken – know	
kirk – church		lang – long	
mon – man		nae – no	
noo – now		tae – to	
twa – two		verra – very	
wean – young child		wee – small	
whit? – what?		wi – with	
ye – you		yon – that/this	

COMMONLY CONFUSED WORDS (1)

affect/effect:

The effects of crap English affect many English speakers.

He affected not to know the difference between affect and effect.

breath/breathe:

A breath of air is what you take when you breathe in.

Breathe deeply, keep taking deep breaths, and I'll give you the bad news.

complement/compliment:

Your hat complements your outfit.

I must pay my compliments to the chef.

defuse/diffuse:

Defuse that bomb – remove the fuse so that it doesn't explode!

If the bomb goes off, the poisonous material inside it will diffuse – it will spread out over a wide area.

THE BOY DONE GOOD:
SOCCER BALLS (1)

Comments from the beautiful game in its often less than beautiful
language.

'Despite the rain, it's still raining here at Old Trafford.'
Jimmy Hill

'It slid away from his left boot which was poised with the trigger cocked.'
Barry Davies

'Manchester United have got the bull between the horns now.'
Billy McNeil

'The run of the ball is not in our court at the moment.'
Phil Neal

'Runners-up at Wembley four times; never the bride
always the bridegrooms, Leicester.'
Peter Jones

'Halifax against Spurs, the original David-against-Goliath confrontation.'
John Helm

'I think you and the referee were in a minority of one, Billy.'
Jimmy Armfield

'So often the pendulum continues to swing with the side that has
just pulled themselves out of the hole.'
Tony Gubba

'Ian Durrant has grown both physically and metaphorically in
the close season.'
Jock Wallace

'I felt a lump in my mouth as the ball went in.'
Terry Venables

IN DEFENCE OF HACKNEYED PHRASES BEGINNING WITH 'B'

We are advised to avoid hackneyed phrases, i.e. those expressions that have become tired through overuse, and lost most of their originality. Often these expressions are so familiar to us that we no longer truly hear them, and while we think we know what is meant by them, we do not genuinely understand what they mean. So if some phrases have become tired, some English speakers have become lazy. For the sake of their often fascinating derivations, at least, these die-hard expressions must surely remain.

'Betwixt the devil and the deep blue sea'
Current meaning: to be caught between two equally dangerous courses of action.
The 'devil' meant here is the seam running along the side of a wooden sailing ship, which was difficult to get to and highly dangerous to be perched on; so it was nothing to do with the chap with red horns holding a pitchfork.

'Beyond the pale'
Current meaning: to be unacceptable.
The Pale was the area of English settlement around Dublin in Ireland in the fourteenth century where English law had to be obeyed. Other 'pales' existed in Scotland, near Calais in France, and in Russia. As 'pale' derives from the Latin word *palus*, meaning a fence, it would seem that to go beyond the pale used to mean to go outside the fence surrounding the Pale, and thus beyond the boundaries of English law and acceptable civilization.

'(the) Bitter end'
Current meaning: until all that is possible has been done.
This expression has negative connotations. 'He'll keep on going to the bitter end' implies that the end may well be unwelcome or sorrowful. However, 'bitter', as used here, has nothing to do with unpleasant feelings or taste, or beer, or weather. In fact, it derives from the word 'bitt', meaning a bollard on the deck of a ship on to which ropes are wound. The end of the cable that is wrapped round the bollard is the 'bitter end'.

(to) Blow hot and cold
Current meaning: to be in favour of doing something at one moment and less keen on it the next.
This phrase derives from the fables of Aesop. One cold day a satyr finds a man trying to warm his fingers by blowing on them. He takes the man home with him and gives him a bowl of hot soup to warm him up. The man blows on the soup in order to cool it, and this enrages the satyr who throws his guest out, wanting nothing to do with a man who can 'blow hot and cold from the same mouth'.

EXPLAIN THYSELF FURTHER

generally	I'm the only person who believes this
I think that	nobody else agrees with me
incidentally	I've just remembered a good story
in my honest opinion	I don't believe a word of this
in the not-too-distant future	it's never going to happen
people think	I don't know what I think
perhaps this means	perhaps it doesn't
reportedly	I need to give my words some extra weight
simply put	everything before has been a lot of waffle
supposedly	this definitely isn't true
the point I am trying to make	no one is listening to me

A LOAD OF OLD BALLS:
SPORTING BLUNDERS

**Sometimes, in the heat of the moment, commentators have been
known to utter the most unfortunate and often nonsensical
statements, leaving the listening audience both amused and bemused.**

'Sure there have been injuries and deaths in boxing – but
none of them serious.'
Alan Minter

'The bowler is Holding, the batsman's Willey.'
Brian Johnston

'He went down like a sack of potatoes, then made a meal of it.'
Trevor Brooking

Rugby: a game of two halves played by gentleman with odd shaped balls.
Anonymous

'The wind always seems to blow against catchers when they are running.'
Joe Garagïola

'I think in international football you have to be able to
handle the ball.'
Glenn Hoddle

'The breeze is getting up and we can just about see Umpire Shepherd's
trousers filling up with wind.'
Jonathan Agnew

'Oh, and here comes Caddick to bowl again from the pavilion end again .
. . well, I don't suppose he'll mind if I read the scores between his balls.'
Henry Blofeld

'This is an interesting circuit because it has inclines. And not just up, but
down as well.'
Murray Walker

IN DEFENCE OF CLICHÉS

Purists may tell us to avoid them like the plague, but what's wrong with a phrase that has been tried and tested by every English tongue? Why not take comfort in the fact that someone else has done the hard work of coming up with words for us? Like Shakespeare, for example. Besides, let someone else take the flak for saying the wrong thing.

The following may be old hat, but often they still hit the nail on the head. So, if you feel so inclined, take the bull by the horns, stick to your guns, jump on the bandwagon and talk the hind leg off a donkey.

Age before beauty.

All's fair in love and war.

Don't bite off more than you can chew.

From bad to worse.

Home is where the heart is.

It never rains, but it pours.

Laughter is the best medicine.

More haste, less speed.

One man's meat is another man's poison.

The pot calling the kettle black.

Like mother, like daughter.

The gods help them that help themselves.

THOUGHTS ON CLICHÉS

'Art doesn't imitate life, if only for fear of clichés.'
Joseph Brodsky

'It's ungrammatical to talk about putting your best foot forward
unless you're a quadruped.'
Lambert Jeffries

'Let's have some new clichés.'
Samuel Goldwyn

'One man's poetry is another man's poison.'
Oscar Wilde

'One man's wage rise is another man's price increase.'
Harold Wilson

'One man's meat is another woman's Sunday gone.'
Mel Calman

'Every Tom, Dick and Harry is named Sam!'
Samuel Goldwyn

'It was always yet the trick of our English nation,
If they have a good thing, to make it too common.'
William Shakespeare, *Henry IV*, Part II

LOVE CLICHÉS

Love makes the world go around.

We can still be friends.

Love is blind.

It's better to have loved and lost than never to have loved at all.

On the shelf.

Don't get mad, get even.

Love hurts.

Unlucky in love.

Marriage is not a bed of roses.

All good things must come to an end.

Too much of a good thing is good for nothing.

CLICHÉD THOUGHTS TO KEEP YOUR SPIRITS UP

Don't worry, be happy!

No news is good news.

Every cloud has a silver lining.

Smile, it makes people wonder what you're up to.

Live and let live.

When one door shuts, another opens.

Que sera, sera.

Today is the first day of the rest of your life.

Zero is sometimes better than nothing.

Always look on the bright side of life.

Shit happens.

SELECTIVE SPORTING CLICHÉS

It's a game of two halves.

You just can't teach that.

He can't quite put it away.

That was a textbook tackle.

He'll never score a better goal than that.

It's a whole new ball game.

That's got to hurt.

They're not out of the woods yet.

It's just too little, too late.

This could get ugly.

The crowd is going wild.

They think it's all over. It is now.

TALK THE TALK:
BUSINESS CLICHÉS

My door is always open.

Time is money.

Nice guys finish last.

Let's get together and touch base.

Keep me in the loop.

Don't move the goalposts.

Money talks. Bullshit walks.

Let's get our ducks in a row.

Give me a ballpark figure.

Keep the train on the tracks.

POLITICAL CLICHÉS

There was a lapse in judgement.

We'll reach across party lines.

I'm sure we can rise above this.

We're here to serve the British people.

Our children's future is at stake.

We'll empower people.

Together we can make this country great.

People will vote with their hearts.

It's time to move forward.

Together, we'll build our future.

We must put this unfortunate chapter behind us.

It's back me or sack me.

MORE LOVE CLICHÉS

The course of true love never did run smooth.

Hell hath no fury like a woman scorned.

I think we should call it a day.

Love at first sight.

Absence makes the heart grow fonder.

Nothing lasts for ever.

There's plenty more fish in the sea.

So many men/women, so little time.

I will survive.

Love conquers all.

DODGY DIALECTS: GEORDIE JAWING

A small selection of words commonly spoken by the people of Newcastle.

av – I've
canna – cannot
dinna – don't
fair-beat – tired out
gannin – going
howay – come on
knaa – know
lang – tall
marra – friend
netty – toilet
peel off – get rid of
reet – right
tellt – told
whey aye – definitely
yem – home

bairn – child
canny – good
divvent – don't
gadgie – man
henna – have not
intiv – into
jaa – to jaw (talk)
mair – more
neb – nose
owa – over
pet – term of endearment
sackless – useless
varra – very
worsels – ourselves
yorsel – yourself

THE BOY DONE GOOD:
SOCCER BALLS (2)

'Oh, he had an eternity to play that ball, but he took too long over it.'
Martin Tyler

'Everything in our favour was against us.'
Danny Blanchflower

'Well, he had two stabs at the cherry.'
Alan Green

'I'm afraid that Francis this season has been suffering from a panacea of injury.'
Dale Barnes

'Manchester United are looking to Frank Stapleton to pull some magic out of the fire.'
Jimmy Hill

'We could be putting the hammer in Luton's coffin.'
Ray Wilkins

'They can crumble as easily as ice cream in this heat.'
Sammy Nelson

'Wilkins sends an inch-perfect pass to no one in particular.'
Bryon Butler

'The Spaniards have been reduced to aiming aimless balls into the box.'
Ron Atkinson

'If you stand still, there is only one way to go, and that's backwards.'
Peter Shilton

'Walsall have given City more than one anxious moment amongst many anxious moments.'
Denis Law

PEARLS OF WISDOM: PROVERBES IN THE ENGLISHE TONGUE

Proverb, *n.* a short pithy saying in general use, which states a general truth or a concise piece of popular wisdom.

All that glitters is not gold.
Beauty is in the eye of the beholder.
Charity begins at home.
Don't put off till tomorrow what can be done today.
Experience is the best teacher.
Feed a cold and starve a fever.
Good men are hard to find.
Half a loaf is better than none.
It's no use crying over spilt milk.
Look before you leap.
Make hay while the sun shines.
No news is good news.
Out of sight, out of mind.
People who live in glass houses should not throw stones.
Revenge is sweet.
Still waters run deep.
The proof of the pudding is in the eating.
Variety is the spice of life.
Where there's a will, there's a way.
You can lead a horse to water, but you can't make it drink.

CONTEMPORARY PROVERBS

A fool and his money are soon partying.

Beauty is in the eye of the beer holder.

Late to bed and early to rise, keeps a twinkle in the eyes.

A thing of beauty keeps you broke for ever.

Soup should be seen and not heard.

All's fair in love and golf.

The proof of the pudding is the box it came in.

All work and no play makes Jack a rich boy.

Where there's a will there's a family at war.

Behind every successful man, there's a woman telling him that he isn't so great.

God help those who are caught helping themselves.

Gossip is the art of letting the chat out of the bag.

KNOW THY MAXIM

Maxim, *n.* a brief statement expressing a general truth or rule of conduct.

He who hesitates is probably right.

He who hesitates has lost the parking spot.

He who hesitates is not only lost, but miles from the next exit.

Commentator: 'Gay sex at sixteen is to be law.'

KNOW THY MANDATE

'There is a mandate to impose a voluntary return to traditional values.'
Ronald Reagan

A clear conscience is usually the sign of a bad memory.

CONTEMPORARY APHORISMS

Aphorism, *n.* a pithy observation which contains a general truth.

A conscience is what hurts when all your other parts feel so good.

If at first you don't succeed, don't admit you ever tried.

Success always occurs in private, and failure in full view.

For every action, there is an equal and opposite criticism.

A conclusion is the place where you got tired of thinking.

Death is Nature's way of telling you to slow down.

Experience is something you don't get until just after you need it.

Hell hath no fury like the lawyer of a woman scorned.

If you must choose between two evils, pick the one you've never tried before.

Life is what happens while you're busy making other plans.

The severity of the itch is proportional to the reach.

To succeed in politics, it is often necessary to rise above your principles.

You never really learn to swear until you learn to drive.

'If at first you don't succeed, failure may be your style.'
Quentin Crisp

CELEBRITY APHORISMS

'A new face is better than a new frock.'
Estée Lauder

'Build a man a fire, and he'll be warm for a day. Set a man on fire, and he'll be warm for the rest of his life.'
Terry Pratchett

'Love is temporary insanity curable by marriage.'
Ambrose Bierce

'Seventy per cent of success in life is showing up.'
Woody Allen

'I can resist everything except temptation.'
Oscar Wilde

'If at first you don't succeed, so much for skydiving.'
Henry Youngman

'The right to suffer is one of the joys of a free economy.'
Howard Pyle, aide to President Dwight D. Eisenhower

BUSHISMS

So many errors in so little time . . .

'They said this issue wouldn't resignate [resonate] with the people. They've been proved wrong, it does resignate.'

'I am a person who recognizes the fallacy [fallibility] of humans . . .'

'The point is, this is a way to help inoculate [?] me about what has come and is coming.'

'The law I sign today directs new funds . . . to the task of collecting vital intelligence . . . on weapons of mass production [destruction].'

'It will take time to restore chaos and order.'

'We cannot let terriers [terrorists] and rogue nations hold this nation hostile [hostage] or hold our allies hostile.'

'A surplus means there'll be money left over. Otherwise, it wouldn't be called a surplus.'

'The illiteracy level of our children are appalling.'

'Well, I think if you say you're going to do something and don't do it, that's trustworthiness.'

'In my line of work you got to keep repeating things over and over and over again for the truth to sink in, to kind of catapult the propaganda.'

'We must all hear the universal call to
like your neighbour as you like
to be liked yourself.'
George W. Bush

CHOOSE YOUR WORDS WITH CARE (1)

'I'm not wearing my wedding ring,' I said with abandon.

'My investments are worth more every day,' said the speculator appreciatively.

'I'm losing my hair,' he bawled.

'How do I keep this fire going?' she bellowed.

'I'm the presenter of *The South Bank Show*,' Melvyn bragged.

'Use your own toothbrush!' she bristled.

'I love the novels of D. H. Lawrence,' said the lady chattily.

'I won't put the Rottweiler down,' the owner declared doggedly.

'You must be my host,' he guessed.

'Stop burning that aromatic substance,' his father said, incensed.

'I love camping,' he said intently.

'Do you call this a musical?' asked Les miserably.

'I love hot dogs,' said the man with relish.

'I wish I'd bought a flat on that street in Paris,' she said ruefully.

'Some you lose,' he said winsomely.

'Your flies are undone,' was the zippy rejoinder.

> 'Too much of a good thing can be wonderful.'
> **Mae West**

MORE CONTEMPORARY PROVERBS

'People who live in stone houses shoudn't
throw glasses.'
Austin O'Malley

All men are born free except at a private maternity hospital.

If the early bird gets the worm, my advice to worms is sleep late.

Charity begins at home, and usually ends up in some
foreign country.

Two is company; three is the result.

A woman's work is never done by a man.

'A hard man is good to find.'
Mae West

Hard work pays off in the future. Laziness pays off now.

An onion a day keeps everyone away.

Diarrhoea waits for no man.

All things come to him whose name is on a mailing list.

'Women should be obscene and not heard.'
John Lennon

ARCHAIC EXPRESSIONS
ARE HERE TO STAY

Blow one's own trumpet.
Diogenes Laertius (third century AD)

Blood is thicker than water.
Euripides (480–c.406 BC)

The wise man will call a spade a spade.
Cicero (106–43 BC)

Two are better than one.
Aristotle (384–322 BC)

Better late than never.
Dionysius (first century BC)

It takes two to quarrel.
Socrates (469–399 BC)

He's an old twaddler with one foot already in the grave.
Plutarch (c.AD 46–c.120)

One man's meat is another man's poison.
Titus Lucretius (c.94–c.55 BC)

If you are at Rome live in the Roman style; if you are elsewhere live
as they live elsewhere.
St Ambrose (c.AD 339–397)

Nothing can be created out of nothing.
Titus Lucretius (c.94–c.55 BC)

Pride goeth before destruction, and an haughty spirit before a fall.
Proverbs, Old Testament

A bird in the hand is worth two in the bush.
Aesop's Fables

A LOAD OF OLD BALLS:
MORE SPORTING BLUNDERS

'He's usually a good puller – but he couldn't get it up that time.'
Richie Benaud

'I love sports. Wherever I can, I always watch the Detroit Tigers
on the radio.'
Gerald Ford

'Argentina are the second-best team in the world . . . and there's
no better praise than that.'
Kevin Keegan

'I never criticize referees and I'm not going to change a habit
for that prat.'
Ron Atkinson

'You might not think that's cricket, and it's not. It's motor racing.'
Murray Walker

'What will you do when you leave football, Jack?
Will you stay in football?'
Stuart Hall

'The first ninety minutes of a football match are the most important.'
Bobby Robson

'Nicolas Anelka – twenty-four years of age, but he's been around
a lot longer than that.'
Kevin Keegan

'Well clearly, Graeme, it all went according to plan, but what
was the plan exactly?'
Elton Welsby

At the end of the day, it's all about what's on the shelf at the
end of the year.'
Steve Coppell

COMMONLY CONFUSED WORDS (2)

either/or / neither/nor:

'By God, Earl, you shall either go or hang.'
King Edward I to the Earl of Norfolk

'By God, O King, I will neither go nor hang.'
The Earl of Norfolk's reply

farther/further:

Before we go any farther, you'll have to have a further look at the map.

gorilla/guerrilla:

The gorilla offered the guerrilla a banana. The guerrilla then shot the gorilla. The other African apes then killed the guerrilla and his friends. So was it gorilla or guerrilla warfare?

hanged/hung:

The well-hung man was well hanged after they put the rope round his neck. They hung a photo of him on the wall, so that no one would forget him.

its/it's:

It's a boy and it looks just like its father.

It's OK to use contractions in colloquial English, but it's a mistake to do so in formal writing.

CHOOSE YOUR WORDS WITH CARE (2)

A truly rural frugal ruler's mural.

The bootblack bought the black boot back.

A dozen double damask dinner napkins.

Fat frogs flying fast.

I'm not the pheasant plucker, I'm the pheasant plucker's mate.

Irish wristwatch.

Lesser leather never weathered wetter weather.

The myth of Miss Muffet.

A pleasant place to place a plaice is a place where a plaice is pleased to be placed.

Pope Sixtus VI's six texts.

Red lorry, yellow lorry.

Six sick slick slim sycamore saplings.

Thieves seize skis.

What time does the wristwatch-strap shop shut?

Which witch wished which wicked wish?

WHY ENGLISH IS BECOMING REDUNDANT

A long time ago, man invented lots of little pictures and symbols to help him communicate with his fellow men. Many thousands of years later, sophisticated spoken languages had developed and replaced these. However, they say that all things come around, or is that full J ? Now, once again, we are becoming a society with no need for words. Instead we communicate by 'drawing' unsophisticated little faces known as smileys or emoticons. Anyway, here's a few, for when you're too tired, lazy, bored or emotional to find the right words to write.

:-)))))	you are very happy	:-D	a big grin
;-)	winking; that's really funny	:-I	you don't care
I-O	bored; yawning; snoring	:-I I	mad
I-I	asleep	:-/	doubtful
:-(	unhappy	>:-(	angry
:-&	tongue-tied	:-@	shouting; screaming
:-C	sad	:'-(	crying
:-O	incredulous	:-X	one's lips are sealed
}:-)	watch out!	B-)	wearing glasses
[:-)	wearing headphones	:-{}	has a moustache
:-)=	bearded	8-)	wearing sunglasses
#:-)	wearing a hat	%-)	drunk
%*@:-(	hungover	:-(~ ~ ~	vomiting
:-~)	runny nose; has cold	((_O_))	big bum
((H))	a hug	:-9	licking one's lips

> If a submarine crew member was to send a text message, would it be a subtext?

SHORTCUTS BY TXT

TXT IS GR8, though it has been known to land some users in hot water over the illicit sending of messages to people other than their respective wives or husbands . . . Here are a few phrases worth trying out.

ALThOsCrvs&MEW/NOBrks	all those curves and me with no brakes
B@TM	busy at the momemt
CntGtEnufOfU	can't get enough of you
DdntIBlOYaMndThsTIm?	didn't I blow your mind this time?
F2T	free to talk
GoTaBASn	gotta be a sin
HlpMEMAkItThruTNIt	help me make it through the night
1nsIsNE	once is never enough
ILTUWotIWanWotIRlERlEWan	I'll tell you what I want, what I really, really want
MAIENDThsSntncW/APropstn?	may I end this sentence with a proposition?
MBA	married, but available
NIcDr$CnITlkUOutOfIt?	nice dress, can I talk you out of it?
RUUP4SxTxt?	are you up for sex text?
Ti2GO	time to go
Zzzz	I'm bored/tired

SIGNS OF THE TIMES

All of these are genuine signs containing examples of crap English, which are either badly written or hilariously nonsensical.

PLEASE GO SLOWLY ROUND THE BEND

PARKING FOR DRIVE-THRU SERVICE ONLY

ANIMALS DRIVE VERY SLOWLY

WOULD THE PERSON WHO TOOK THE STEP LADDER
YESTERDAY PLEASE BRING IT BACK OR FURTHER STEPS WILL BE TAKEN

AFTER TEA BREAK STAFF SHOULD EMPTY THE TEAPOT AND STAND
UPSIDE DOWN ON THE DRAINING BOARD

CAUTION AUTOMATIC DOOR PUSH TO OPERATE

WHEN YOU CAN'T SEE THE SIGN THE RIVER IS UNDER WATER

AUTOMATIC WASHING MACHINES: PLEASE REMOVE ALL YOUR CLOTHES
WHEN THE LIGHT GOES OUT

WE PROVIDE THE LOWEST PRICES AND WORKMANSHIP

**THIS DOOR IS
NOT TO BE USED
AS AN EXIT
OR AN
ENTRANCE**

LAUGHABLE LABELLING

Strange though it may be, these highly unnecessary and somewhat pointless warnings and instructions have appeared on genuine products.

Do not iron clothes on body.

For indoor and outdoor use only.

Serving suggestion: defrost.

Why not try tossing over your favourite breakfast cereal. [on a packet of raisins]

Objects in the mirror are actually behind you. [on a cyclist's helmet-mounted mirror]

Sliced ham with vegetarian cheddar.

Whole chicken medium fresh.

Peel tomatoes easily by standing in boiling water.

Keep out of children. [on a Korean kitchen knife]

100% pure all-natural fresh-squeezed juice from concentrate.

SHOPPING THE SHOPPING HORRORS

Nonsensical shop-window notices, all written according to the rules of crap English.

Open seven days a week and weekends.

Broken lenses duplicated here.

Rare, out-of-print and non-existent books.

Wonderful bargains for men with 16 and 17 necks.

Seasonal toilet rolls.

And now, the superstore unequalled in size, unmatched in variety, unrivalled inconvenience.

Now is your chance to have your ears pierced and get an extra pair to take home, too.

Same-day cleaning. All garments ready in 48 hours.

One-hour photos. Collect tomorrow.

Soft and genital bath tissues or facial tissues 89 cents.

Semi-annual after-Christmas sale.

We do not tear your clothing with machinery. We do it carefully by hand.

We will oil your sewing machine and adjust tension in your home for $1.00.

Used Cars. Why go elsewhere to be cheated? Come here first.

Prize-winning sausages. Once tasted, you'll never want another.

'FOR SALE' NOTICES: HOW DID THESE GET BUY?

It is hoped that the quality of the products being sold was better than the quality of this selection of notices which advertised the items for sale.

Snow blower for sale . . . only used on snowy days.

For sale. Three canaries of undermined sex.

Free puppies . . . part German shepherd, part dog.

Toaster: a gift that every member of the family appreciates. Automatically burns toast.

Free: farm kittens. Ready to eat.

Christmas tag sale. Handmade gifts for the hard-to-find person.

Amana washer $100. Owned by clean bachelor who seldom washed.

For sale: Braille dictionary. Must see to appreciate! Call Jerry.

Must sell: 3 grave spaces, very reasonable. Plus air conditioner.

German shepherd. 85 lbs. Neutered. Speaks German. Free.

For sale. Antique desk suitable for lady with thick legs and large drawers.

Have several very old dresses from grandmother in beautiful condition.

For sale. Instant coffee table.

Great Dames for sale.

THERE'S A JOB GONE

It pays to think a little before drafting a job advertisement, otherwise the replies you receive may be rather surprising . . .

Three-year-old teacher needed for pre-school. Experience preferred.

Central Otago stud farm requires single young man.

Secretarial/Clerical – Excellent word-processing and typing skills. Conscious, creative and detail-oriented.

Man wanted to work in dynamite factory. Must be willing to travel.

Our experienced Mum will care for your child. Fenced yard, meals, and smacks included.

Man, honest. Will take anything.

Mother's helper needed – peasant working conditions.

Wanted. Preparer of food. Must be dependable, like the food business, and be willing to get hands dirty.

Wanted. Widower with school-age children requires person to assume general housekeeping duties. Must be capable of contributing to growth of family.

Wanted. Hair cutter. Excellent growth potential.

Part-time help wanted. Must have creative skills, driving licence and car with outgoing personality.

> Tired of cleaning yourself?
> LET ME DO IT.

MORE SIGNS OF THE TIMES

CAUTION: WATER ON ROAD DURING RAIN

GBH FITNESS CLUB

BABY AND GARAGE SALE

PLEASE TAKE ADVANTAGE OF THE CHAMBERMAID

KEEP DOOR CLOSE

FOOTPATH UNSUITABLE FOR PEDESTRIANS

IT IS FORBIDDEN TO DROP HITCHHIKERS
ON THE MOTORWAY

BOTTOMLESS PIT 65 FEET DEEP

SHEEP, PLEASE KEEP DOGS UNDER CONTROL

IN THE BEGINNING THE WORD WAS GOOD

Some people adhere to the belief that literary standards have fallen due to less time spent reading the Bible. Is that so? Judging by the thought put into the writing of these religious-based signs and notices, it might not necessarily be the case.

The third verse of 'Blessed Assurance' should be sung without musical accomplishment.

Due to vandalism in the churchyard we must ask anyone with relatives buried here to keep them in order.

A bean supper will be held in the church hall. Music will follow.

Eight new choir robes are currently needed, due to the addition of several new members and to the deterioration of some old ones.

Due to the Rector's illness, Wednesday's healing services will be discontinued until further notice.

Will the last person to leave please see that the perpetual light is extinguished.

Persons are prohibited from picking flowers from any but their own graves.

Our thanks are due to Miss Goodman who laboured the whole evening at the piano, which once again fell upon her.

'If English was good enough for Jesus Christ,
it's good enough for me.'
**A US congressman to Dr David Edwards, head of the
joint National Committee on Language, about the necessity for
a commercial nation to be multilingual**

MALAPROPISMS

Malapropism, *n.* a mistaken use of a word in place of a similar-sounding word, which often produces inadvertent amusement. The term comes from Mrs Malaprop, a fictional character in Richard Sheridan's eighteenth-century play *The Rivals*, who was famous for her misapplication of words.

Good punctuation means not to be late.

He had to use a fire distinguisher.

It will percushion the blow.

Dad says the monster is just a pigment of my imagination.

Isn't that an expensive pendulum round that man's neck?

She was a child progeny, you know.

He winched a little as she began to stitch the wound.

He's a wolf in cheap clothing.

My sister has extra-century perception.

A sneer went up after the Prime Minister's speech.

She's got such a big nose, she'll need a blow job if she wants to make it in Hollywood.

A boxer is a sportsman who always hurts the one he gloves.

> 'I would like to thank Nasal Beard for that warm welcome.'
> **George W. Bush, thanking Hazel Beard**

FANS OF MRS MALAPROP

'President Carter speaks loudly and carries a fly spotter, a fly
swasher – it's been a long day.'
Gerald Ford

'This is unparalyzed in the state's history.'
Gib Lewis, Texan politician

'Republicans understand the importance of bondage between
a mother and child.'
Dan Quayle

'He was a man of great statue.'
Thomas Menino, Mayor of Boston

'We must rise to higher and higher platitudes together.'
Richard J. Daley, former Mayor of Chicago

'It is beyond my apprehension.'
Danny Ozark, baseball team manager

'She's really tough; she's remorseful.'
David Moorcroft

'Be sure and put some of those neutrons on it.'
Mike Smith, ordering a salad at a restaurant

'It ain't the heat; it's the humility.'
Yogi Berra

'I am providing you with a copulation of answers to several
questions raised . . .'
**Former Mayor of Washington, DC, Marion Barry,
in a letter to a constituent**

PROOFREADING PAYS

Did you know that . . .

. . . in 1631, an edition of the King James Bible was printed with the error: 'Thou shalt commit adultery'?

. . . a biography of George Eliot was published, referring to the author as 'he' throughout?

. . . the first edition of *Ulysses* by James Joyce is believed to contain more than 5,000 typographical errors?

> 'Out came the nun and smacked him in the face.'
> ***Typographical error in an autobiography –***
> ***'nun' should have read 'sun'***

SPELL CHECK, SPELL CHECK, SPELL CHECK

One would like to think that dictionaries and spell-checkers are dependable tools, but they won't always help us out. Watch out for words that sound the same. They may be spelled correctly, but are they right?

Mrs Jones hated flying, but she tried to steal herself for the flight to Spain.

The policeman said that the murdered girl was a died blonde.

Soup? Sandwich? Chile?

It was like a damn broke, and she cried and cried.

Faint hart never one fair lady.

When a night one his spurt.

His week voice spoiled the opera.

If Lewis Carroll were alice today.

Michelangelo painted the Sixteenth Chapel.

The children sang 'Away In A Manger' as the shepherds arrived.

> 'She peed at her reflection in the mirror.'
> *Typographical error in a romantic, historical novel*

POOPER-SCOOPS:
UNFORGETTABLE HEADLINES

Sometimes newspapers are so quick to make headlines that they lose the plot. Watch your words, or you may find yourself scooping up that poop.

Astronaut Takes Blame For Gas In Spacecraft

Blind Woman Gets New Kidney From Dad She Hasn't Seen In Years

Chef Throws His Heart Into Helping Feed Needy

Deaf Mute Gets New Hearing In Killing

Enraged Cow Injures Farmer With Axe

Filming In Cemetery Angers Residents

Golfer Charged With Drunken Driving

Hospitals Are Sued by 7 Foot Doctors

Infertility Unlikely To Be Passed On

Juvenile Court To Try Shooting Defendant

I CAN SEE CLEARLY NOW THE BRAIN HAS GONE

The following are genuine sentences taken from students' essays and exam papers.

'Ancient Egypt was inhabited by mummies and they all wrote in hydraulics.'

'Moses led the Hebrew slaves to the Red Sea, where they made unleavened bread, which is bread made without any ingredients.'

'The dodo is a bird that is almost decent by now.'

'Socrates died from an overdose of wedlock.'

'Charles Darwin was a naturalist who wrote the organ of the species.'

'A triangle which has an angle of 135 degrees is called an obscene triangle.'

'Johann Bach wrote a great many musical compositions and had a large number of children. In between he practised on an old spinster which he kept up in his attic.'

'Moses went up Mount Cyanide where he was given the Ten Commandments.'

'Three kinds of blood vessels are arteries, vanes and caterpillers.'

'The process of turning steam back into water again is called conversation.'

LOOK IT UP!

Some words which are most frequently looked up in online dictionaries.

UBIQUITOUS	ESOTERIC
PARADIGM	SERENDIPITY
OBSEQUIOUS	ECLECTIC
DICTIONARY	PRAGMATIC
JINGOISM	FOIBLE
IDIOM	OXYMORON
EFFECT	HUBRIS

FUN WITH A PUN

Pun, *n.* a joke based on the exploitation of a) the different possible meanings of a word, or b) the existence of two or more words that sound the same but have different meanings; generally described as a 'play on words'.

Do bakers with a sense of humour bake wry bread?

Why do people go to live in France? They have nothing Toulouse.

How do we know that Farmer Brown was good at his job? He was outstanding in his field.

The politician had to slash the budget, so he held a fund razor.

The farmer decided to get a cow, and milk the idea for all it was worth.

Working as a lift operator has its ups and downs.

There was ghost at the hotel so they called for an inn spectre.

Two parts of an eye were discussing which made better puns. Their debate raged until one said to the other, 'You, my friend, are simply the pupil. I am by far the cornea.'

A punster entered a local paper's pun contest. He sent in ten different puns in the hope that at least one of the puns would win. Unfortunately, no pun in ten did.

> 'Hanging is too good for a man who makes puns;
> he should be drawn and quoted.'
> **Fred Allen**

PRESSING PUNS

Burning Questions On Tunnel Safety Unanswered
About the possibility of fires in the Channel Tunnel

Science Friction
About an argument between scientists and the British government on the topic of BSE or mad-cow disease

Waugh Cry As Aussies Blast Off
About Steve Waugh, the Australian cricketer

Return To Gender
About a reccurrence of sexual harassment in London post offices

On A Whinge And A Prayer
On the resignation of a minister of the British government

Officials Say Atoll Do Nicely
About the fraudulent sale of small Pacific islands

PLAY ON WORDS, PLAY ON

Birthday candles are for people who want to make light of their age.

They accused her of stealing the brooch, but they just couldn't
pin it on her.

I'd rather have a bottle in front of me than a frontal lobotomy.

Girls are like pianos. When they're not upright, they're grand.

I am nobody. Nobody is perfect. Therefore, I must be perfect.

What is better than presence of mind in a railway accident?
Absence of body.

> 'You will have written exceptionally well if, by skilful arrangement of your words, you have made an ordinary one seem original.'
> **Horace**

CORRECT WORD ORDER MAKES ALL THE DIFFERENCE

Fried fresh fish,
Fish fried fresh,
Fresh fried fish,
Fresh fish fried,
Or fish fresh fried?

THE FOUR MOST IMPORTANT WORDS IN THE ENGLISH LANGUAGE

I
ME
MINE
MONEY

THAT'S AN UNDERSTATEMENT

'. . . It's no big thing to me . . .'
J. R. Triplett, a retired lorry driver, after winning $239 million in the Virginia state lottery.

IS THERE A LANGUAGE DOCTOR IN THE HOUSE? (1)

Based on the madness of some of these examples, let's hope that medical staff pay more attention to patient care than they do to the accuracy and quality of their medical notes.

Both breasts are equal and reactive to light and accommodation.

The patient has been depressed ever since she began seeing me in 1983.

Odour of alcohol on breast.

The patient has no past history of suicides.

Examination of genitalia reveals that he is circus sized.

The patient is tearful and crying constantly. She also appears to be depressed.

The patient left the hospital feeling much better except for her original complaints.

The patient refused an autopsy.

By the time he was admitted, his rapid heart had stopped and he was feeling better.

Comes to Emergency Department complaining of vaginal breathing.

Between you and me, we ought to be able to get this lady pregnant.

On the second day the knee was better and on the third day it had completely disappeared.

COMMONLY CONFUSED WORDS (3)

lie/lay/laid/lain/lying:

'Lie down,' ordered one of the two men pointing their guns at him, 'and lay down the gun!' He laid his gun at his captor's feet and lay down on the floor. Lying there, he wondered if this would be the same as the time he had lain there for two days, only that time there were the others lying alongside him. His hat lay next to him. He would be lying if he weren't wishing it was his gun lying there. He continued to lie there for several days longer than he lay there last time.

older/elder/oldest/eldest:

His elder brother is older than my brother, who is my elder by ten years. I don't know which is the elder of his two sisters. Actually, I think Jane is the eldest of the three siblings.

The elder, which is a tree with white flowers and dark berries, is the oldest tree in the forest.

precede/proceed:

I proceeded to say that A precedes B in the alphabet.

'Dawn precedes dusk,' I said, as I proceeded on my way in the early hours.

He proceeded against them for libel.

queue/cue:

The man stood in a queue to buy a snooker cue.

As the queue in the bank grew longer, another till opened on cue.

The actress hovered in the wings as she awaited her cue.

TROUBLE WITH BODY PARTS

'His brain was going as quick as his legs and he was in two minds.'
Alan Brazil

'She gives the players a shoulder to talk to.'
Neil Webb, of the England football team's faith healer

'He's holding his right arm and signalling with his left.'
John Motson

'Businessmen should stand or fall on their own two feet.'
Edwina Currie

'Novotna's holding her nerve – her nerve, of course, has always been her Achilles heel.'
John Barratt

'He is putting his mouth where his hopes are!'
Sky Sports commentator

'He has those telescopic legs that can turn a Leeds ball into an Arsenal one.'
John Motson

'That's a wise substitution by Terry Venables: three fresh men,
three fresh legs.'
Jimmy Hill

'He's pulling off defenders' shoulders and making it difficult
for them!'
Kevin Keegan

' . . . and you could see Parnevik's heart visibly drop.'
Peter Alliss

'The boys' feet have been up in the clouds since the win.'
Alan Buckley

'Ian Rush unleashed his left foot and it hit the back of the net.'
Mike England

'If Gower had stopped that [cricket ball] he would have
decapitated his hand.'
Farokh Engineer

POOPER-SCOOPS: MORE UNFORGETTABLE HEADLINES

Kids Make Nutritious Snacks

Limbless Hit Out At Rise In Living Costs

Mine Strike Ballet To Go Ahead

New Jersey Judge To Rule On Nude Beach

One-legged Man Competent To Stand Trial

Panda Mating Fails; Veterinarian Takes Over

Queen Mary Having Bottom Scraped

Red Tape Holds Up New Bridge

Stiff Opposition Expected to Casketless Funeral Plan

Two Sisters Reunited After 18 Years At Checkout Counter

Use Of Heroin Shooting Up

Victim Tied, Nude Policeman Testifies

Workers Finish Boring Sewer Tunnel

**Man Struck By Lightning
Faces Battery Charge**

IS THERE A LANGUAGE DOCTOR IN THE HOUSE? (2)

Patient has chest pain if she lies on her left side for over a year.

Patient has left his white blood cells at another hospital.

She stated that she had been constipated for most of her life until 1989 when she got a divorce.

Patient had waffles for breakfast, and anorexia for lunch.

Patient has two teenage children, but no other abnormalities.

She has had no rigours or shaking chills, but her husband states she was very hot in bed last night.

Patient was becoming more demented with urinary frequency.

Patient was seen in consultation by Dr X, who felt we should sit on the abdomen and I agree.

When she fainted, her eyes rolled around the room.

The patient states there is a burning pain in his penis which goes to his feet.

The patient was in his usual state of good health until his airplane ran out of gas and crashed.

The patient was to have a bowel resection. However, he took a job as a stockbroker instead.

She is numb from her toes down.

The patient will need disposition, and therefore we will get Dr Ward to dispose of him.

While in the emergency room, she was examined, x-rated and later sent home.

THE WRITING IS ON THE WALL

Some worthwhile graffiti

BREAKFAST IN LONDON
LUNCH IN NEW YORK

– British Airways

... AND LUGGAGE IN BERMUDA

**WHISKAS – NINE
OUT OF TEN OWNERS
SAID THEIR CATS
PREFERRED IT**

BESTIALITY – NINE OUT OF
TEN CATS SAID THEIR
OWNERS PREFERRED IT

NOTHING WORKS FASTER THAN ANADIN

IF NOTHING WORKS
FASTER THAN ANADIN
– USE NOTHING

WALLS HAVE EARS

I JUST FOUND ONE
IN ONE OF THEIR
PORK PIES

AS EASY AS ABC:
AN A-TO-Z OF SIMILES

Simile, n. a figure of speech in which one thing is likened to another dissimilar thing by the use of the words 'like' or 'as' to give particular emphasis.

The English language has countless examples of such comparative phrases, some more wacky than others ...

As agile as a monkey
Cries like a baby
Eats like a pig
As gentle as a lamb
As innocent as a lamb
As light as a feather
As nutty as a fruitcake
As proud as a peacock
Like a ray of sunshine
Like two peas in a pod

Like a bat out of hell
As dry as a bone
As fat as a pig
As hard as nails
As keen as mustard
As mad as a March hare
As obstinate as a mule
As quick as lightning
As sick as a parrot
Like a wet weekend

TEN SINFUL SIMILES

You may say that the above examples are as old as time; that they are like worn shoes or comfortable slippers. Here are some more contemporary examples.

1. As baffled as Adam and Eve on Mother's Day
2. As bald as a baboon's arse
3. Noisy like a skeleton on a tin roof
4. As old as the Dead Sea when it was only ill
5. As premenstrual as a tampon with a lit fuse
6. Rare like rocking-horse shit
7. As tight as a camel's arse in a sandstorm
8. As useful as a grave robber in a crematorium
9. As welcome as a fart in a spacesuit
10. As much use as a chocolate teapot

METAPHORICALLY SPEAKING

Metaphor, *n.* a figure of speech in which one thing is likened to another, different thing by being spoken of as if it were that other.

'I am the astronaut of boxing. Joe Louis and Dempsey were just jet pilots. I'm in a world of my own.'
Muhammad Ali (who understood literal meaning)

She had a special place in his heart.

Education is a gateway to success.

On the road to peace.

Life in the fast lane.

His mind was caged by depression.

She followed in her mother's footsteps.

She had returned from the edge of death.

He was hitting his head against a brick wall.

The detective had wrapped up the mystery.

'It's like a game of chess: all the cards are thrown in the air, the
board's turned over and you're in a whole new ball game.'
Michael Howard

TEN MIXED METAPHORS

Mix metaphors, *vb.* to use two or more inconsistent metaphors in a single expression.

1. Strike while the iron is in the fire.

2. You can kiss that down the drain.

3. I'll deal with that road when we cross it.

4. We're cooking on all cylinders now.

5. It's an open-and-dry case.

6. The storm of protest was nipped in the bud.

7. In the dead of summer.

8. We've got the best of both sides of the coin.

9. Never kick a good horse in the mouth.

10. We don't want to lead them up the garden path and then pull it from under them.

METAPHORIC MIX-UPS

'Keep a stiff upper chin.'
Samuel Goldwyn

'He put all his eggs in one basket and pulled out a cracker.'
Dennis Taylor

'That's just the tip of an ice cube.'
Neil Hamilton

'The local authorities are caught between the deep blue sea of the rates and the frying pan of the Poll Tax.'
Conservative MP

'It will create an excitement that will sweep the country like wildflowers.'
Samuel Goldwyn

'It is a red-hot political football!'
ITN reporter

' . . . You've been playing with fire and now you're reaping the whirlwind.'
Dr Ian Banks

'Unless somebody can pull a miracle out of the fire, Somerset are cruising into the semi-final.'
Fred Trueman

'The gelling period has just started to knit.'
Ray Wilkins

'When I see the pictures they play in that theatre, it makes the hair stand on the edge of my seat!'
Samuel Goldwyn

ENGLISH ENGLISH PLEASE! (1)

Though the American public generally remain true to the English
language – both in its use and abuse – some English words have been
overlooked and replaced by alternatives, just to confuse matters.

American	English
apartment	flat
baby carriage	pram
bathroom	loo/toilet/lavatory/bog
can	tin
chopped beef	mince
cookie	biscuit
diaper	nappy
elevator	lift
eraser	rubber
fanny	backside
flashlight	torch
fries	chips
gas	petrol
highway	motorway
I neglected to say	I forgot to say
jello	jelly

> 'Quotation: the act of repeating erroneously
> the words of another.'
> **Ambrose Bierce, _The Devil's Dictionary_**

WRITE IT RIGHT, TELL IT AS IT SHOULD BE TOLD: COMMON MISQUOTATIONS

Those who find it difficult to remember 'famous' quotations may take comfort in the idea that it is gentlemanly to get one's quotations wrong. Educated people should be familiar with the wit and wisdom of great writers and thinkers, but should not cite them word for word, as this demonstrates not only a lack of interpretation, but vulgar superiority. In other words, it's showing off. However, if you think that this is a lot of bosh, or you are the type to enjoy correcting others, make sure you know the right words off pat.

Wrong: Pride goes before a fall.
Correct: Pride goeth before destruction, and an haughty spirit before a fall.

Wrong: All power corrupts.
Correct: Power tends to corrupt and absolute power corrupts absolutely.

Wrong: Blood, sweat and tears.
Correct: Blood, toil, tears and sweat.

Wrong: Fresh fields and pastures new.
Correct: Tomorrow to fresh woods and pastures new.

Wrong: To gild the lily.
Correct: To gild refined gold, to paint the lily.

Wrong: By the skin of my teeth.
Correct: I am escaped with the skin of my teeth.

Wrong: Thin red line.
Correct: Thin red streak, tipped with a line of steel.

Wrong: A little knowledge is a dangerous thing.
Correct: A little learning is a dangerous thing.

Wrong: My lips are sealed.
Correct: My lips are not yet unsealed.

Wrong: Money is the root of all evil.
Correct: The love of money is the root of all evil.

> 'It is a good thing for an uneducated
> man to read books of quotations.'
> **Winston Churchill**

SO YOU THINK THEY WROTE GOOD?

Even the most famous and successful writers have been accused of failure where their use of the English language is concerned.

'He splits his infinitives and fills them up with adverbial stuffing. He presses the passing colloquialism into his service. His vast paragraphs sweat and struggle; they could not sweat and elbow and struggle more if God himself was the processional meaning to which they sought to come . . .'
H. G. Wells on Henry James

'The ineffable dunce has nothing to say and says it with a liberal embellishment of bad delivery, embroidering it with reasonless vulgarities of attitude, gesture and attire. There never was an impostor so hateful, a blockhead so stupid, a crank so variously and offensively daft. He makes me tired.'
Ambrose Bierce on Oscar Wilde

'He has never been known to use a word that might send a reader to the dictionary.'
William Faulkner on Ernest Hemingway

'Poor Faulkner. Does he really think big emotions come from big words?'
Ernest Hemingway on William Faulkner

'The Doctor has a transcendental gift, when he is writing sense, for making this appear to be nonsense . . .'
Edith Sitwell on F. R. Leavis

'Why don't you write books people can read?'
Nora Joyce to her husband, James Joyce

'With the single exception of Homer, there is no eminent writer, not even Sir Walter Scott, whom I can despise so entirely as I despise Shakespeare when I measure my mind against his . . . It would positively be a relief to me to dig him up and throw stones at him.'
Robert Browning

'I have tried lately to read Shakespeare, and found it so intolerably dull that it nauseated me.'
Charles Darwin

FOREIGN ECONOMY

Sometimes our Continental neighbours say it so much more succinctly, which highlights the more verbose tendencies of the English language.

Continental	English
à la carte	on a menu, separate, or individually priced dishes, not part of a set meal
bête noire	a thing or person one dislikes very much
carte blanche	full power to act as one thinks best
Doppelgänger	a ghostly double or counterpart of a living person
enfant terrible	a person who causes shock or offence because of their controversial or indiscreet behaviour or ideas
femme fatale	a dangerously attractive and seductive woman
grande dame	a woman of influential position in a particular field
milieu	a person's social environment
objet d'art	a piece of art or decoration, regarded as a work of artistic value
raison d'être	the most important reason for a person or thing's existence
schadenfreude	malicious enjoyment of other people's misfortunes
vis-à-vis	with regard to, compared to
Weltanschauung	a conception of the world and of humanity's relation to it
Zeitgeist	spirit of the times; trend of thought and feeling in a particular period of time

FOREIGN EXCHANGE (1)

Many words in the English language are open to misinterpretation, particularly by non-native speakers. What follows is a selection of amusing examples of alternative translations.

allotment	full of meaning
autocue	traffic jam
autonomy	I should be recognized by him
avoidable	what a bullfighter tries to do
baloney	where hemlines fall
barbecue	waiting in line for a haircut
bicycle	go shopping for two wheels
burglarize	what a crook sees with
campaign	backache from sleeping too long in a tent
contest	exam with rigged questions
counterfeiters	workers who put together kitchen cabinets
counter intelligence	knowing how to knock down price tags
control	a short, ugly prison inmate
dilate	live long
dogmatic	run by canine power

COMMONLY CONFUSED WORDS (4)

rack/wrack:

The wrack from the shipwreck was all over the beach. Jim was racked with guilt that he hadn't been able to warn the sailors.

He racked his brains, but still couldn't remember where he'd put the spice rack.

sight/site:

The site where I intend to pitch the tent tonight is just in sight.

'That's a sight for sore eyes!' he said as the camping site came into view.

thank you/thankfully:

Thank you for your thank-you letter, but not for writing thankyou as one word.

'The post is here,' I cried thankfully.

I thank you for pointing out that thankfully does not mean luckily, but thankfully its usage is changing and hopefully thankfully will soon be accepted.

who's/whose/whom:

Who's that man whose car has been clamped?

To whom does that child belong?

your, you're:

You'll find you're forgetting your own name next.

Don't count your chickens.

You're the best in the world. No, you are, really.

SPOONERISMS

The Reverend William Archibald Spooner (1844–1930) had a highly active brain which raced so quickly that his tongue could not keep up with his thoughts. This often resulted in an unintentional switching of the initial sounds in two or more words, which produced a phrase entirely different to the one that he had intended. For example, he once meant to say 'well-oiled bicycle' but instead said 'well-boiled icicle', and when intending to refer to Queen Victoria as the 'dear old Queen' he called her the 'queer old dean'. Thus was born the 'spoonerism'.

Pre-Spoonerism	Spoonerism
butterfly	flutter by
ease my tears	tease my ears
funny bone	bunny phone
take a shower	shake a tower
lunatic	tuna lick
a pack of lies	a lack of pies
rattle your cage	cattle your rage
flat battery	bat flattery
lighting a fire	fighting a liar
a headless bird	a bedless herd
it's pouring with rain	it's roaring with pain
our loving shepherd	our shoving leopard
hot wheels	what heels
save the whales	wave the sails
lying dog	dying dog

POTENTIALLY UNFORTUNATE SPOONERISMS

(NOT ATTRIBUTED TO REV. SPOONER)

It's *The Tale of Two Cities*.

Sir, you are certainly a shining wit.

Have you brought your sleeping bag?

She is sure pretty.

He fills her soul with hope.

Have you seen her sick duck?

He's not a pheasant plucker.

She showed me her tool kits.

He's a smart fella.

Oh, the suffering of purgery on my soul!

Fire truck.

The acrobats displayed some cunning stunts.

BE MORE-OR-LESS SPECIFIC

Confusion over numbers is very common, apparently – it's easy to lose count and forget the basics, as these laughably bad examples prove.

'Walking down the street, I saw – to be perfectly precise – ten, twenty, fifty, one hundred beggars . . .'
Tommy Boyd

'But the main group is just a few yards behind the main group . . .'
Brendan Foster

'We've had drivers going off left, right and centre . . .'
Murray Walker

'The single most important two things we can do . . .'
Tony Blair

'I can't promise anything but I can promise 100 per cent.'
Paul Power

'In two words, impossible.'
Samuel Goldwyn

'It was a game of three halves.'
Steve Davis

' . . . and with eight minutes left the game could be won or lost in the next five or ten minutes.'
Jimmy Armfield

'The World Cup is every four years, so it's going to be a perennial problem.'
Gary Lineker

'When you restrict a side to 170, ninety-nine times out of ten you feel confident.'
Michael Atherton

ABOUT RIGHT

Sure, the next train has gone ten minutes ago.

Her head moved from side to side, nodding fiercely.

She had just made it to her door when the car that had been following her caught up with her and shot her in the back.

She landed spreadeagled in a ball.

He stood his ground, fists curled, legs akimbo.

He could tell she was puzzled. She was frowning with her eyebrows.

He could tell she was angry. She was clenching her teeth.

ENGLISH ENGLISH PLEASE! (2)

American	English
line	queue
mail	post
movie theater	cinema
overpass	flyover
pacifier	dummy
pants	trousers
parking lot	car park
period	full stop
potato chips	crisps
sidewalk	pavement
trunk	boot
vacation	holiday
vest	waistcoat
windshield	windscreen
zip code	postcode

FOREIGN EXCHANGE (2)

eclipse	what a Cockney barber does for a living
enema	not a friend
fortunate	consumption of expensive meal
gargoyle	olive-flavoured mouthwash
heroes	what a guy in a boat does
isolate	me not on time
knowledge	nothing to stand on
legend	a foot
lymph	walk with a lisp
munchkin	when cannibals eat their family
nitrate	cheaper than day rate
pecan	container in which to urinate
protein	in favour of youth
relief	what trees do in the spring
support	drink fortified wine

'What's another word for thesaurus?'
Steven Wright

BE MORE-OR-LESS SPECIFIC AGAIN

'There are only four cars on the circuit at the present moment and two of them are in the garage.'
Murray Walker

'I feel that this is my first year, that next year is an election year, that the third year is the mid point, and that the fourth year is the last chance I'll have to make a record since the last two years . . .'
Dan Quayle

'It's become a fascinating duel between three men.'
David Coleman

'Just under ten seconds . . . call it nine point five in round figures.'
Murray Walker

'You give 100 per cent in the first half of the game, and if that isn't enough in the second half you give what's left.'
Yogi Berra

'That is what has made America last these past 200 centuries.'
Gerald Ford

'Except for his car, he's the only man on the track . . .'
Murray Walker

'If crime went down 100 per cent it would still be fifty times higher than it should be.'
Councilman John Bowman (commentating on the high crime rate in Washington, DC)

'Baseball is 90 per cent mental –
the other half is physical.'
Yogi Berra

VERBAL BANANA SKINS

'He's going up and down like a metronome.'
Ron Pickering

'The police are not here to create disorder, they're here to preserve disorder.'
Richard J. Daley, former Mayor of Chicago

'Nobody goes there any more; it's too crowded.'
Yogi Berra

'I went up the greasy pole of politics step by step.'
Michael Heseltine

'Marie Scott . . . has really plummeted to the top.'
Alan Weeks

'You could literally hear the silence fifty miles away.'
Simon Bates

'You can almost taste the cedarwood from the oak barrels.'
Oz Clarke

'He's doing the best he can do – he's making the worst of a bad job.'
Fred Trueman

'You have reached the turning point on a voyage of no return.'
Simon Bates

'You should always go to other people's funerals;
otherwise, they won't come to yours.'
Yogi Berra

SINGULAR OR PLURAL?

None is attractive to me and none are attracted to me.

Neither is attractive to me, but either are willing.

The majority of English speakers is guilty of saying the majority of English speakers are guilty.

The public is aware that the public thinks it are not getting English right.

The first person, the second person and the third person agrees that subject and verb are subject to change.

The English faculty is excellent and in possession of all their faculties.

The audience was bored and as a result they were restless.

The company is confident that the company were right.

Government is concerned that the government were put in a difficult position.

AND THE SINGULAR IS . . .

Well, these unlucky thirteen don't have one.

ALMS
CATTLE
DOLDRUMS
EAVES
PANTS
SCISSORS
TROUSERS

BRACES
CLOTHES
IDES
MARGINALIA
PLIERS
SHORTS

AND THE PLURAL IS . . .

One Englishman, a bore; two Englishmen, a club; three Englishmen, an empire.

One Irishman, a drinker; two Irishmen, a fight; three Irishmen, partition.

One Frenchman, a lover; two Frenchmen, an affair; three Frenchmen, a ménage.

One German, a burgher; two Germans, a beer-parlour; three Germans, an army.

One American, a businessman; two Americans, a market; three Americans, a cartel.

One Italian, a tenor; two Italians, a duet; three Italians, an opera.

One Russian, an anarchist; two Russians a chess game; three Russians, a revolution.

One Japanese, a gardener; two Japanese, a cult; three Japanese, electronics.

ADVERB OR ADJECTIVE?

The boy did good.
The meal tastes well.
The girl talks posh.
I speak English fluent.
Lately, the speaker arrived.
He ran to the accident quick.
I ran to the scene fastly.

'What if I had said, instead of
"We shall fight on the beaches",
"Hostilities will be engaged with our
adversary on the coastal perimeter"?'
Winston Churchill

WHY GET HET UP ABOUT
THE PASSIVE?

Well, the wrong thing was said and the wrong thing got written.

Because standard English is thought to be in decline.

English was broken. English was fixed.

He was made to write it out again. It was then thought to be correct.

Each of Shakespeare's plays uses fine writing.

MORE VERBAL BANANA SKINS

'The President is going to lead us out of this recovery.'
Dan Quayle

'Outside the killings [Washington] has one of the lowest crime rates in the country.'
Marion Barry, former Mayor of Washington, DC

'I get to go to lots of overseas places, like Canada.'
Britney Spears

'. . . The wind shining, and the sun blowing gently across the fields.'
Ray Laurence

'I have made good judgements in the past. I have made good judgements in the future.'
Dan Quayle

'It was impossible to get a conversation going; everybody was talking too much.'
Yogi Berra

'An end is in sight to the severe weather shortage.'
Ian McCaskill

'We're going to have the best-educated American people in the world.'
Dan Quayle

'Your ambition – is that right – is to abseil across the English Channel?'
Cilla Black

MORE CONFUSING WORDS (1)

akimbo:

If you are standing akimbo, you are standing with your hands on your hips and your elbows turned outwards. Your legs may be astride or apart, but even a contortionist would have trouble standing legs akimbo.

bear/bare:

I cannot bear to think of you barely escaping from that bear, and how unfortunate that you were bare at the time.

He decided to bare his soul to his friend, and tell him he could no longer bear a grudge.

chronic/acute:

I have had chronic backache for a long time, but I have had acute appendicitis only once.

Chronic does not mean bad, as I'm sure you are acutely aware.

There is an acute shortage of good teachers, due to the government's chronic mismanagement of education.

conscience/conscious:

She was conscious that her conscience had been pricked by the guilt she was feeling.

After lying in a coma for a week, the patient was now conscious.

NOW THEN, OXYMORONS . . .

Oxymoron *n.* a figure of speech in which opposite ideas are combined; a smart saying which at first appears foolish – or foolish smart.

The fart at the **free trade** conference caused a **deafening silence**; everyone was **clearly confused** as to who had done it. Everyone tried to **act naturally**, although the boy in the corner was a **definite maybe**.

Everyone said they enjoyed the **sweet tart**, although it was an **open secret** that the **larger half** of the guests thought it tasted terrible.

The huge spot on the end of his nose was **seriously funny**, although everyone did their best to maintain a **blank expression** in his company.

She was **pretty ugly** and he wasn't sure he liked the fact that they were **alone together**.

The **original copies** of Mrs Brown's home videos had been **found missing**. It was **cold comfort** to her that they were discovered in Mr Green's shed.

A **minor crisis** occurred when it was discovered that **plastic glasses** had been brought out for the **dry wine**.

The **crash landing** was a **near miss** as far as the houses near by were concerned. By the time it hit the press, however, the story was **old news**.

Although **nothing much** was said about it at the time, it was reported as the most important archaeological find in **modern history**.

The pathologist let out a **silent scream** when she realized that the dead man was **still moving**.

It was an **awfully good authentic replica**. It was a **genuine imitation**.

MODERN PARLANCE: TRENDY TERMINOLOGY, VOGUE WORDS AND EPHEMERAL EXPRESSIONS

blamestorming — sitting around a boardroom table discussing what went wrong and who was to blame

ego-surfing — searching the World Wide Web for your own name

fake bake — spray-on or sunbed tan

flyboarding — estate agents' practice of putting 'For Sale' or 'Sold' signs outside houses that are not for sale, as a way of encouraging new business

going postal — meaning to lose it, to be unable to deliver the goods

irritainment — entertainment that is annoying but at the same time compelling

lavender language — language associated with the gay community

metrosexual — heterosexual male with a strong interest in clothes, hairstyle, beauty products, cooking and home accessories

middle youth — time of life for people aged between thirty and forty-five who do not acknowledge middle age

mouse potato — a person who is on-line all the time or who plays computer games continually

sex up — to spice up something in order to make it seem more exciting than it is

slackademic   someone who spends too much time in further education, rather than getting a job

speed-dating   saving time in the search for a partner by engaging in a brief chat with all the other singletons in the room at an organized event

starter marriage   a short-lived first marriage that ends in divorce with no children, no property and no regrets

sunset clause   the final endpoint to a contract, business deal, or other legislation; something that stops negotiations going on indefinitely

treeware   any printed publications e.g. newspapers and books

tweenagers   children between the ages of eight and twelve who emulate their teenage counterparts

tweenie pound   economic potential of such children

MORE OXYMORONS

almost exactly

constant variable

death benefits

exact estimate

freezer burn

hot chilli

jumbo shrimp

modern history

non-working mother

paid volunteer

safety hazard

skinny broad

taped live

tragic comedy

virtual reality

business ethics

criminal justice

even odds

extinct life

genuine imitation

ill health

living dead

natural additives

only choice

rolling stop

same difference

sweet sorrow

tight slacks

unbiased opinion

working holiday

MORE CONFUSING WORDS (2)

different from/different than/different to:

The Americanisms 'different than' and 'different to' are different from the correct English form 'different from'.

desert/dessert/deserts:

When his camel ran off into the desert, he was forced to desert his dessert and go after it. As he had not tied the animal securely, everyone said he had got his just deserts.

elude/allude:

I allude to the troubles in Africa, and those who have managed to elude them. I also allude to the word elude, the meaning of which eludes me.

forward/foreword:

I was looking forward to speaking to him about the foreword to the book. It might be a bit forward of me, but I wanted to point out areas that could be improved.

grate/great:

Please clean out the grate. The fireplace doesn't look great with soot all over it, and it grates that I'm the only person who cares about this.

Please be careful how you move the grate, however, because it makes a terrible grating sound if you drag it.

It's just great that you grated that mouldy cheese with my new cheese grater. It really grates, when you do things like that.

TO REALLY BE SPLITTING INFINITIVES, THIS IS HOW YOU MUST REALLY BE USING THEM

To properly split infinitives you have to put a word between the word 'to' and the following verb. Some just sound better than others.

to ably walk	to actually help
to boldly go	to coldly stare
to gladly help	to hardly hear
to suddenly understand	to rudely burp
to awfully feel	to vulgarly say
to frightfully cost	to disgustingly smell
to revoltingly eat	to expensively cost
to precociously talk	to fastidiously pick

COMMON INTERJECTIONS

ah, aha, ahem, attaboy, bingo, cheers, crikey, dear dear, egad, eh, golly, gosh, good heavens, ha-ha, heigh-ho, hem, hey, hey presto, hi, ho hum, hurray, jeez, lackaday, lordy, my word, oh, ooh, oops, ouch, ow, phew, phooey, rats, righto, shoot, tush, tut-tut, ugh, uh-huh, uh-oh, voilà, well well, wow, yikes, yippee, yoicks, zoinks

THE OLD ONES ARE ALWAYS THE BEST

Old bankers never die, they just lose interest.

Old cardiac surgeons never die, they just get bypassed.

Old deans never die, they just lose their faculties.

Old farmers never die, they just go to seed.

Old geometry teachers never die, they just go off on a tangent.

Old journalists never die, they just get depressed.

Old kings never die, they just get throne away.

Old lawyers never die, they just lose their appeal.

Old magicians never die, they just disappear.

Old nitpickers never die, the just feel lousy.

Old pilots never die, they just go to a higher plane.

Old quarry workers never die, they just get blasted.

Old robbers never die, they just steal away.

Old sculptors never die, they just lose their marbles.

Old tree surgeons never die, they just pine away.

Old upholsterers never die, they just don't recover.

Old veterinarians never die, they just go to the dogs.

Old wheelfitters never die, they just get retired.

AITCHES 'ONESTLY DROPPED

'It ain't the 'unting as 'urts 'im,
it's the 'ammer, 'ammer, 'ammer
along the 'ard 'igh road.'
Punch (1856)

An erb
Hideous Americanism – 'a herb' in English

The letter H is a problem letter. On the one hand, a great many English speakers cannot pronounce it; on the other, those that abhor the dropping of an aitch cannot resist treating the letter like a vowel. For example, why do people feel the need to write 'an hotel'? One certainly won't end up in an 'ostel without it, because there is no grammatical rule governing the 'an'; it has merely an 'istory.

An 'abitual offender of this type of writing may not be aware that although 'an' was formerly favoured before an unaccented syllable beginning with the letter H, now that the H in these words is pronounced, there is really no need for it. So 'a' will do nicely.

If you must ask for **an** hotel room at the reception desk, be advised that you should refrain from aspirating the H. It's make-your-mind-up time: an 'otel or a hotel?

A tip for those in the habit of losing the first letter of such words such as 'ouse, 'er, 'im and so forth, is that there is really no need to find it for the word honour, which, strangely, non-standard-English speakers very often do. 'Onour' not 'honour' on this occasion, please.

Hermine
French for ermine

'He was sojourning at an hotel in Bond Street.'
Anthony Trollope

MORE CONFUSING WORDS (3)

lead/led:

He led me to the stationery cupboard where I found lead pencils.

I was in the lead until I fell over the lead piping.

loose/lose:

Things become loose and you lose them. So that they do not get lost, tighten up the loose things, and then you won't be a loser.

less/fewer:

These days fewer people seem to know that 'fewer people' is correct and not 'less people'.

Less sugar was wanted in general, but Mrs Jones specifically wanted fewer sugars in her tea.

practice/practise:

'I must practise getting to my practice on time,' said the doctor.

Practise your tennis. Go to tennis practice.

principal/principle:

The college principal was against it in principle.

My principal fear was that I'd lose my principles.

write/rite/right/wright:

Please write about the rites of courtship in the medieval romance.

Get it right and know your rights!

The playwright based his play on a wheelwright's feud with a shipwright and a wainwright.

ALL THINGS SAID AND DONE

'Every once in a while, you let a word or phrase out, and you
want to catch it and bring it back. You can't do that.
It's gone, gone for ever.'
Dan Quayle

'They have been at a great feast of languages,
and stolen the scraps.'
William Shakespeare, *Love's Labour's Lost*

'I stand by all the misstatements that I've made.'
Dan Quayle

'Say what you have to say and the first time you come to a
sentence with a grammatical ending – sit down.'
Winston Churchill

CONCLUSION

Anyone this far into the book will now have a clear idea of just how
crap and confusing English can be. But, above all, he/she/they will
also have an understanding of what great fun it can be . . . when you
break the rules. Remember, English is like an omelette – to make it
you have to break some e.g.s.

BIBLIOGRAPHY

Burchfield, R. W., *The New Fowler's Modern English Usage* (Oxford University Press, 1996)

Gowers, Ernest, *The Complete Plain Words* (HMSO, 1986)

Green, Jonathon, *The Slang Thesaurus* (Penguin, 1999)

Jarman, Colin, *I Said it My Way: The Guinness Dictionary of Humorous Misquotations* (Guinness, 1994)

Rees, Nigel, *Cassell's Dictionary of Word and Phrase Origins* (Cassell, 2002)

Safire, William, *On Language* (Times Books, 1981)

Safire, William, *What's The Good Word?* (Avon Books, 1982)

Trask, R.L., *The Penguin Guide to Punctuation* (Penguin, 1997)

FURTHER READING

LUVTLK?: Ltle bk of luv txt, Michael O'Mara Books Ltd

Outrageous Expressions, Michael O'Mara Books Ltd

Shite's Unoriginal Miscellany, Michael O'Mara Books Ltd

The Total TXTMSG Dictionary, Michael O'Mara Books Ltd

WAN2TLK?: Ltle bk of txt msgs, Michael O'Mara Books Ltd

Wicked Cockney Rhyming Slang, Michael O'Mara Books Ltd

The World's Stupidest Signs, Michael O'Mara Books Ltd

More of the World's Stupidest Signs, Michael O'Mara Books Ltd

INDEX

The index for this book is based on the Dewey Decimal system, reference 808*.

Common Errors in English